Choices
and
Wheels

CAROLYN J. NEWCOMBE

ISBN 978-1-63961-402-8 (paperback)
ISBN 978-1-63961-403-5 (digital)

Christian Faith Publishing
832 Park Avenue
Meadville, PA 16335
www.christianfaithpublishing.com

Printed in the United States of America

Ascribe to the Lord the glory due His name;
Bring an offering and come before Him.
Oh, worship the Lord in the beauty of holiness!
—1 Chronicles 16:29

Trust in the Lord with all your heart,
And lean not on your own understanding;
In all your ways acknowledge Him,
And He shall direct your paths.
—Proverbs 3:5–6

Dedicated to
Helen Bishop Newcombe.
Her Adventurous spirit
brought her to Troy, New York.
Met the love of her life.
Together they instilled in their
four children a zest for life.

FOREWORD

by Beverly Woodcock

The day Carolyn Newcombe was born, the Lord gave us all an inspiration. He gave us a person whose intelligence, whose faith, and whose courage shines through. Carolyn's character can be seen in vignettes. The old grainy family movie of the Newcombes from the fifties, with Dr. Newcombe, Helen Newcombe, Vaughn, Glen, and Beverly all running around in their bathing suits and Carolyn floating like a water spider in a lake. A college graduation when the entire audience rose as one to give Carolyn a standing ovation as she wheeled across the stage to receive her bachelor's degree. A scene at the White House on July 26, 1990, when President George H. W. Bush signed into law the Americans with Disabilities Act, extending civil rights protections to millions of Americans with disabilities and changing lives forever, a law Carolyn believed in, fought for, and like most things she puts her mind to, made happen.

Where does Carolyn get her drive, her iron will, her character? Certainly from her accomplished father, who left her life all too early, and from her brothers and sister, who refused to treat her differently, who supported her, who literally lifted her up, and who did not spare her from sibling teasing. Then there was Helen, Carolyn's mother. There has never been a mother who loved a child more than Helen loved Carolyn. Helen's love was born of pride for what Carolyn had accomplished, and worry for what lay in store for her when Helen was no longer there.

Helen had every right to worry. But she need not have. Carolyn was bound to do well. Carolyn has the strength of character, the gift of faith, the sense of fun and optimism, and the iron-clad determination to make her own way, to carve out her own life, to make her own friends, and to declare her own independence.

This is the Carolyn Newcombe we all know. A person who has accepted the gift of life with humor and humility, who wheels her way through life in the shadow of the divine, and who marks her days not as obstacles to overcome but as opportunities to be realized.

INTRODUCTION

For the LORD does not see as man sees; for man looks at
the outward appearance, but the LORD looks at the heart.
—1 Samuel 16:7b

While writing this book, several times I thought to
myself, "Why are you bothering? Nobody will be
interested in reading it." Discouragement is common to
most humans. We humans have many characteristics and
emotions in common. It took me a long time to figure
this out. While growing up, I looked at life through a lens
of having a disability. Slowly, as time passed and our culture changed, my view of my disability has become less
dominant.

A disability does give you a perspective on certain
things. Any person perceives circumstances differently
depending on their experiences in life. Sprinkled throughout the book are stories of the reaction of individuals to
my particular disability, cerebral palsy. The last third of the
book has some chapters written by friends to give you, the
reader, another prospective.

Recently, I attended a "celebration of life" service for
a man, Dave. For as long as I knew him, he had to walk

slowly and deliberately with crutches. He was a kind man, willing to lend his technical services to anyone. Among the many testimonials, several individuals commented that he always refused help. One particular person got my dander up when he described an encounter with Dave where, after Dave politely refused help, the person brought a Walmart scooter to Dave. The man's intentions were well-meaning, but for many people with disabilities, his actions would be considered irritating, some would say disrespectful.

My purpose in writing this book is twofold—to demonstrate that God can and does use anyone, whether they have a disability or not, to accomplish His purposes and to give you a tiny taste of life living with a physical disability. My prayer is that your view of life will be enriched and that your view of people with disabilities will be expanded.

1

Hurricane

For You formed my inward parts;
You covered me in my mother's womb.
I will praise You, for I am fearfully and wonderfully made;
Marvelous are Your works.

—Psalm 139:14

The wind was blowing the afternoon and evening of August 31, 1954, increasing in velocity as the day went on. Sometime during that period, Helen must have asked Dick to take her to the hospital.

She was about to have their fourth child. She was three weeks past her due date and probably very anxious to give birth, but time dragged on without any sufficient action going on. She became concerned about their other three children. There was a hurricane going on out there, and Glen and Bev, the two younger ones, might need at least one of their parents.

Helen was left alone in a room for a period, which, in retrospect, was not wise. Her labor became difficult. The hospital called Dick to tell him there were complications. As I understand it, the doctor in charge, at some point that evening, asked my father, "Who do you want to be saved, the mother or the baby?" I don't know his reply, and it doesn't matter, because both my mother and I lived long and joyful lives.

My dad named me Carolyn Jean. Contrary to what some think, I wasn't named after Hurricane Carol, which raged outside. It seems more than a coincidence that my middle name is the same as his younger sister, Betty (Elizabeth Jean).

The medical profession calls the type of birth my mother had a breach birth, which means my feet came out first. The umbilical cord was wrapped around my neck, causing a lack of oxygen to the brain. My father rushed his baby girl to a hospital in Hartford, which was an hour away, where they placed two needles in my brain.

I don't know my parents' first reaction to giving birth to a baby who, more than likely, would have severe disabilities. Were they disappointed they didn't have a "normal" infant? Were they angry, anxious, or just sad? More than likely, they anxiously wondered what my disability would be like. While cleaning out Mom's house many years later, I found a letter from her mother. In it she expressed her sympathy and stated it was a tragedy. It never occurred to me to ask Mom what her initial reaction was.

I will never know their first reaction, but it doesn't matter. From the very beginning, I was engulfed in love. I didn't have the natural ability to suck, so Mom used an eyedropper to feed me. What patience she had!

My earliest memories were of my mother rocking me near the pantry door in the huge kitchen, softly singing, "If you ever go across the sea to Ireland, and maybe at the closing of the day, you'll sit and watch the moon rise over Claddagh, and see the sun go down on Galway Bay."

Sometime during my first year of life, probably within the first two or three months, a doctor recommended that my parents put me in an institution. There happened to be one in the next town. This was a common practice in the first half of the twentieth century. Big brick buildings were built, usually in rural areas, to house children and adults who had physical and or mental disabilities, the majority of whom were classified as mentally retarded.

It's my suspicion that after the initial emotions had diminished, Dad did research on the latest treatments for cerebral palsy, my diagnosis. So, unlike many parents during that era, when the doctor made the recommendation to place me in an institution, my parents were prepared with their answer, no. They also knew in their hearts they couldn't give up their child. They knew by looking into my eyes there was potential in me.

2

Family Foundations

Honor your father and your mother,
that your days may be long upon the land which
the LORD your God is giving you.
—Exodus 20:12

The foundation of my life began in the hallway of a hospital in the foothills of the Adirondack Mountains in Troy, New York. A young Canadian nurse, Helen Elizabeth Bishop, met an internist in the new field of radiology. Richard Vaughan Newcombe was born in Burlington, Vermont, on September 9, 1916. His father, Eugene, was a Yankee railroad man, and his mother, Maude, took in laundry to wash to make ends meet.

I imagine their first few dates, which might have been few and far between, would have involved going to places where local bands were playing. It was the "big band" era, and they soon found out they enjoyed dancing together. They discovered they had many other things in common. Not only their interest in the medical field, but good books and love of nature and exploring. They might have chuckled if they had the opportunity to introduce their siblings to one another; they both had brothers named Jack.

Of course, they quickly established that they were the same age. Born in the same year (Helen on August 15), they were only three weeks apart in age. But every once in a while, Dick, Richard's nickname, teased her throughout their marriage about being older than him.

Helen was the oldest daughter of ten children. Being raised on a farm on St. Joseph Island, she had her share of responsibilities taking care of the younger children. There were the twins, Blanch and Murry; Dot, who was so tiny a gust of wind would blow her over; and Joyce, the youngest and who also became a nurse. Calvin, Maurice, Milton, and Jack must have helped their father with the difficult day-to-day farmwork. Eventually, all but Milton scattered throughout Canada or the United States.

Dick was from a much smaller family. He had an older half-sister, Jeri (Jeraldine), whose mother passed away in later years. Jeri would marry and settle down in New Jersey. In later years, Helen and Jerry would meet in New York City for a Broadway show or classical concert and catch up on family news.

Dick's younger sister, known as Betty, was a sweet, sensitive woman whom Helen got to know in the early part of her marriage. Because of her sensitive nature, Dick and Helen talked Betty out of her great desire to become a nurse. She might have regretted listening to them. She eventually married Jim Crabtree and in the midsixties moved to Saint Louis, Missouri, with their two young sons, Tom and Jim.

Dick and Helen had a small ceremony of marriage in Massachusetts on July 26, 1941. They lived in the Boston area while Dick completed his internship at the Mayo Clinic. Being an astute man, he anticipated the United States entering World War II and made plans accordingly. As soon as he graduated, he volunteered to be in the Medical Core.

Like many men of that era and throughout history, he wanted to ensure he left his mark on the world but knew winds of war were blowing. While overseas serving his country, his first son was born on September 21, 1942. He received the news in the Army mail in a letter from Helen with a small picture of her holding Richard Vaughan Newcombe II. In his younger years, Richard went by various nicknames, including Skip, which his grandfather (Dick's dad) called him because he loved to skip around when he was a toddler. Eventually he settled on going by his middle name, Vaughan.

After the war, Dick and Helen started looking for a radiology partnership. They seriously considered a partnership in California. Instead, they settled in Mansfield, a small town in Northeastern Connecticut in 1948. That same year, their second son was born, Glen Bishop. Many years later, when their children discovered this, they contemplated how much different life would have been growing up in California.

3

Early Years

Train up a child in the way he should go,
And when he is old he will not depart from it
—Proverbs 22:6

Like most individuals, I only remember glimpses of memories of the early years of life. In a way, I did most activities children do, swim, play hide-and-seek, go downhill sledding, and even skate. This was way before any adaptive sports equipment, so my dad had to be creative.

Due to having cerebral palsy, my balance and coordination are greatly affected. I've spent my life in a sitting position. I was six when I received my first wheelchair. Before then, I got around by rocking in a child-size rocking chair. Dad drilled a long bolt in the center of the seat and padded it. When someone placed me in the rocking chair, they would put my legs on either side of the bolt.

Dad had the same concept in mind when he designed a sled. He took a store-bought wooden sled, built a back and sides on it, and put a bolt where my upper thighs would be.

So when the family went sledding down the hill and into the field at the back of the house, Dad would put me on his shoulders piggyback-style, holding my wrists, as we walked up the snow-covered hill. Actually, I think Mom stayed inside to get a little peace. One of my brothers would carry the sled up the hill, Dad would seat me securely in the sled and give me a shove. It was always an adventure to see how far across the field I would go.

Ice-skating was enjoyable, being outside in the fresh cold winter air put a spark in all of us. There was a pond in the woods a little distance from the hill we went sledding on. When we got to it, I sat on the sled, and each family member would take turns pulling me around the pond by a long rope that was attached to the sled. Skating was more Mom's speed, so sometimes she would join us.

Board games, mind puzzles, and books were an essential part of the Newcombe household. Heaven knows how many times Mom read *Make Way for Ducklings, Snow White and the Seven Dwarves,* and the list could go on. As I grew older, she took the time to read longer, more mature books such as *The Secret Garden, Charlotte's Web, Stuart Little*, and many others. She instilled in each of her children the love of reading and the sense of adventure and learning through books.

I remember sitting on my dad's lap, watching him teach either Vaughan or Glen to play chess. He explained the different directions each of the pieces could move and described various possible moves. Although I was young, I must have absorbed something; years later when I was dating Ken, my first love, we played our first game of chess and I won. His pride must have been hurt because he never asked me to play chess again in the five years I knew him.

A game of Monopoly was a frequent occurrence in our house, sometimes lasting for hours. Someone would move my piece around the board for me and throw the dice, but I would make the decisions, smart or otherwise, when choices had to be made. I don't remember winning too many Monopoly games, but considering my competition, it's not surprising. In adult life, Vaughan became a certified public accountant, Glen had a successful retail business for over thirty-five years, and Bev obtained her master's degree in governmental affairs from Colombia University.

Since my family loved the outdoors, another adventure we enjoyed together was going to Lake Titus in upstate New York. My dad's half sister, Jeri, and her husband, Bill, owned an unheated cabin, which they let various family members use. We went up to their cabin in the summer for two or three weeks. With an aluminum boat tied to the roof and the station wagon stuffed with clothes and supplies, we made the long trek to the cabin.

One year we brought Bev's cat. Bev was a cat lover, although Mom and I weren't too far behind. All the way up and back that year we heard, "Meow, meow!" I woke up in the middle of the night once that year and saw this black creature on four legs walking across the partition that separated the bedrooms. Not realizing what it was, I screamed. Mom came, and after calming me down, we figured out it was our feline friend.

I remember Dad taking me out on the lake in the aluminum boat, just him and me. He put my canvas seat attached to a metal frame on the bottom of the boat, revved the engine, and off we went.

On the other hand, unusual things like physical therapy were an everyday occurrence for me throughout my childhood and young adult life. The brains of young children who have cerebral palsy have to be "trained" to do what comes naturally to the average youngster. The objective of most physical, occupational, or speech therapists is to obtain the optimal functional ability of the person he or she is working with, which is many times unknown.

Mrs. Ahern was my first physical therapist. She did a lot of patterning, moving my legs in a walking motion so my brain would get the idea of how to walk, and moving my arms up and down to prevent muscles from getting too tight and eventually becoming unusable. She taught Mom to do the same.

What made my relationship with Mrs. Ahern unusual was our families were friends; in fact, for a time, we were next-door neighbors. Her children were about the same ages, so we spent hours together playing in the hay in the barn, board games, and such.

Many times, children with disabilities need to have surgeries to repair something; depending on the disability, surgeries can be numerous. I was no exception. When I was five, I had surgery to release my hamstrings on the back of my knees. This surgery was a common procedure for children with cerebral palsy. For six weeks my legs were straight out in front of me as I sat in a wooden wheelchair at Newington Children's Hospital.

From age seven to thirteen, I spent the academic year at Newington Children's Hospital, which had one wing set up as a school. Some classrooms had two grades combined, like third and fourth, while others had one grade. For some reason, I only remember being in second and sixth grade. If my memory is correct, I was in second grade two or three times. This was not because of any academic reason but because some of the teachers didn't want someone with my severity of disability. The majority of the children were there for some kind of corrective surgery on their backs for scoliosis, Legg-Perthes, which required the child to be in a brace with their legs spread wide for six months, or a variety of other conditions. It didn't bother me that I didn't attend those grades, but once in a while, I would become curious and wander into the classroom when nobody was around just to see what it was like.

Mrs. Glidden, the teacher I had the most during those years, made learning fun. She loved holidays and always decorated her classroom. One of her favorites was Flag Day, June 14, a day originally established by a schoolteacher to celebrate the birthday of the Stars and Stripes. She took this opportunity to get all the children in her classroom outside for a ceremony and a little fresh air. This was no small task because most of her pupils were either in a bed on wheels or used a wheelchair. Fortunately for her, she had a balcony attached to her classroom that a few beds could be rolled out onto.

She went beyond her duties as a teacher and led a Brownie and Girl Scout troop once a week in the evening. She included her daughter, Marybeth, in the troop. We did most of the activities other troops did; recite the pledge, do learning activities to earn badges, and my favorite, sing songs. Today this would be considered a segregated setting and would be frowned upon, but back then we thought nothing of it.

A major part of my time at Newington Children's Hospital was taken up by occupational and speech therapies. Newington was a teaching hospital. Not only did they have physical and occupational therapy students from the University of Connecticut observe and work with me individually, but groups of doctors and interns would come to observe and learn. Some of the children, including me, would demonstrate their abilities, or disabilities, as the case may be, in our underwear.

As you can imagine, this wasn't my favorite thing. First, we had to wait, sometimes for what seemed like hours, for our time in the spotlight, then we would need to demonstrate something like getting on our hands and knees. I would get nervous as the doctors would dissect my position, the way I held my head, and so on. No permanent mental health damage was done. You did what was required of you.

Sometimes exercises would extend into the evening. Several of us would push around on a flat, padded wooden board with small wheels to build up our muscles. Of course, we would race up and down the long hallway.

Newington was unique in that all the children on two of the units went home every weekend. This meant Mom would drive over a two-and-a-half-hour round trip on Friday and Sunday afternoons. She did this without any complaints from her lips. Her dedication allowed me to participate in family life.

4

Dad

Jesus wept.

—John 11:35

Lying in bed on Good Friday in 1963, I heard hushed voices downstairs. Bev and I shared a bedroom since we moved to the house next door a year or so earlier. Mom had said a prayer, which included starving children in Africa supported by our church. A little while later I heard footsteps on the stairs, then someone turned the corner and entered the room. It was Dr. Anderson.

Dr. Anderson was an old-fashion community pediatrician who was always smoking a pipe, or so it seemed. He and his family were friends of ours. Many Thanksgiving dinners were spent feasting at their house.

On this night, he had unexpectedly dropped by the house, so Mom had him come upstairs to check out a cough I was having. He came in the room, took a quick look with his tiny flashlight down my throat, and gave me a pat, saying, "You'll be fine." But there was an unusual sadness in his demeanor.

Dr. Anderson's unexpected visit brought news that would have reverberations for years to come. On the way home from a medical meeting in Boston, Dad was driving on a curvy road and hit a tree head-on. It was reported he died instantly.

As an eight-year-old child, I didn't understand the implications this would have on each member of the family. All I knew was Dad was in heaven and I wouldn't see him anymore. In Sunday school, we read simple Bible stories; some of them told about Jesus making a way for people to go to heaven.

The next day was spent at Lisa's, a friend who was the same age as me. Her parents had bought the house we used to live in before we moved. We colored Easter eggs, but my heart wasn't in it. Lisa practiced playing the piano, which I usually enjoyed, but that day, not so much. Reflecting back, I think I just wanted to be with my family, but Lisa's mom probably kindly offered to take me for the day.

Seven months later, on November 22, we learned of the assassination of President John F. Kennedy, and I watched with the nation the public mourning that followed. There was the contrast between the very public mourning of President Kennedy and the very private mourning of my family. Throughout the years, I oddly linked the two in my mind. Watching Kennedy's two children on TV, I would wonder if they would remember their father from their own mind or just from the myriad of information concerning their famous dad. They both were younger than me.

Mom would keep Dad's memory alive by once in a while telling tidbits of stories. One of her favorites demonstrated his dry sense of humor mingled with his medical background. He couldn't understand "why it had to be bronchitis, it should be purplechitis." She also told of his early years growing up in Burlington. Being the oldest son, some of the punishments his father dealt were a bit harsh. As a boy, sometimes he would sleep on the porch in the dead of winter with the snow blowing in.

Although Mom lived over forty years longer, she never remarried. There were one or two potential suitors, but she would kindly tell them she wasn't interested. Her loyalty was for her husband and him alone.

Like millions of others who have lost their fathers at an early age, every so often throughout the years, I would wonder what life would be like if Dad were around. What would he think of me? How much different would life be? The answers were unknowable.

In my childhood and well into my adult life, I struggled with the holy days of Good Friday and Easter. Oh, I knew the events: Jesus riding into Jerusalem on a donkey, the Last Supper where Judas Iscariot betrayed Him, His agony in the garden, the crucifixion, Mary at the tomb, and the resurrection. Although I believed these events occurred, there was always a gray cloud of sorrow over them. For one thing, why was it called "Good" Friday? Only after a personal encounter with Jesus and His wisdom, slowly revealed over time, would the events of the Holy Week come to have a glorious meaning for me.

5

1964

My brothers, show no partiality as you hold the
faith in our Lord Jesus Christ, the Lord of glory.

—James 2:1

For many people, some years of their lives stand out
more than others. The year 1964 was one of those for
me. For one thing, I completed my first decade.

The world's fair was in New York City that year, and
my family was fortunate to have an aunt and uncle, Dad's
brother Jack (given name of Eugene) and his wife, Trip
(given name of Barbara), who lived just outside the city
in Rye. They had four children, Laura, who was Bev's age,
Scott, Polly, who was my age, and Todd, who was a year or
two younger. Our families got together two or three times
a year. Usually, Jack's family came up to Connecticut to
get out of the city for a few days. He was a writer for *Life*
magazine at the time. On this occasion, we traveled down
to their house for a few days.

While attending the 1964 World's Fair, Mom had arranged that each of my siblings would take turns pushing me in my wheelchair around the fairgrounds. I had my eyes on some rides like those cable baskets that were above our heads, crossing the whole fairground. It looked so fun to be up there. Yes, I was able to see the fair from above ground level.

Soon my siblings figured out there was an advantage to being with me. Naturally, there were long lines for different rides. On a few occasions, we were pulled out of line and escorted to the front of the line or a side door to get on the ride faster and to assist in accommodating my disability. Disney's "It's a Small World" boat ride was particularly memorable. Sometimes I still hear the song in my head.

But there was one place that wasn't so accommodating. We had stood in line in the hot sun when a man in a uniform motioned to us to get out of line and follow him. He said that particular ride was too dangerous for me and sent us on our way. Looking back, I consider that incident my first encounter of blatant discrimination. Oh, I have had many people stare at me before. Mom taught me to be polite to individuals who stare, saying they are just curious and indicated I should get used to it. So I smile and sometimes say, "Hi." Although I don't get as many stares now, I still use the same tactic and found it's effective at disarming someone. They tend to become embarrassed and walk away, but I never got comfortable having people look at me. This incident was at a different level, although I didn't realize it at the time.

*****

The *Ed Sullivan Show* was a staple variety show on TV every Sunday evening for millions of Americans in the '50s and '60s. He usually had a new comedy routine, puppet show, or musical bands, but on February 9, most young people exploded with excitement when they were introduced to the Beatles that night. The girls in the ten-bed ward at Newington Children's Hospital were no exception. Watching the black-and-white TV, which was mounted high on the wall above our heads, we were in awe of them. After the show was over, there was a great deal of chatter among my friends, but as usual, I just listened. Little did we know they, along with other bands and political forces, would change the world forever.

6

Sheila

She seeks wool and flax,
and works with willing hands.
—Proverbs 31:13

For most of us, there are people we will never forget. Sheila Timson was one of those people in my life. She had wavy salt-and-pepper hair, which she curled with big pink curlers. How she slept on those things was beyond me.

She was like a grandmother to me. My maternal grandmother lived a distance away on a tiny island in Canada above the Great Lakes. The only vague memory I had that was connected to her was the time Mom had to leave unexpectedly to go to Canada and put my siblings in charge of taking care of me. This was an unusual occurrence. I have no recollection of my father's parents.

Sheila and her husband, Tommy, lived in a little brown house at the back of ours. She worked at the American Thread Company, which manufactured spools of thread in Willimantic. But soon after Sheila and Tommy moved into the house, my parents began to wonder how stable Tommy was. Although arrangements had been made that Sheila would give Mom a break in taking care of me, concerns must have developed when it was discovered Tommy had a drinking problem. He might have become jealous of me for the amount of time Sheila would spend with me. Eventually, they got divorced, which was a relief to all.

Many hours I would spend in that little brown house with a potbellied stove in the living room. Although the living room stayed toasty warm in the winter, the two bedrooms were on the chilly side due to a lack of insulation. We played card games such as crazy eights and cribbage, but by far our favorite was rummy. Sheila would hold two sets of cards in one hand, one the regular way and the other between her index and middle finger, with the suits facing me. I would indicate the cards I wanted to put down to make a run, like the jack, queen, and king of hearts, by the movement of my head and eyes. Sheila would keep score and whoever got to 500 first won the game.

One of the bedrooms also functioned as a sewing room. I enjoyed watching her sew. She encouraged me to help her by letting me move the big round knob on the right of the tan sewing machine. My gross motor skills enabled me to do this and other tasks. This knob was connected to the bobbin. She would control the fabric and the thread while I made the bobbin go up and down. Sometimes she would place the foot pedal, which also controls the bobbin, on the table for me to press the button. Although this method was faster and easier, the threads and the fabric would also get messed up faster and easier. There seems to be an analogy to life here that takes a lifetime to learn.

Sheila loved to pamper me. Every week she would give me a manicure. This included soaking my nails in the bathroom sink for five minutes, pushing back cuticles, and cutting and filing my nails. Sometimes I would stay overnight with her, sleeping in the same bed with pink satin sheets. She told me they were supposed to be luxurious, but I found them slippery, especially keeping my head on the pillow.

There is no doubt Sheila would have done anything for me, but as I grew older, I thanked God she wasn't my mother. She would have spoiled me rotten.

When Windham Heights, an apartment complex for people who have low incomes, was built in 1973, Sheila moved there. This move increased our growing apart.

One Friday evening three years later, after driving me home from an hour away, Mom sat down on the blue couch in the living room and told me in a matter-of-fact voice that Sheila had a stroke the day before. She had fallen, and by the time someone found her, it was too late. I burst out crying.

My tears were not only for the loss of my dear friend but also tears of anger. Why did Mom wait so long to tell me? And why was she so calm? My young mind didn't consider she had already lost both of her parents and her husband. To me, she was being insensitive.

To make things worse, Mom said Sheila's last wishes included no funeral or memorial service. I found this hard. There was no outlet for my emotions. No way to say goodbye. I came to realize the tradition of funerals were for the living, not the dead. But why didn't she want a service? Did she believe in God, or was there something in her past? It might have been a combination of both. On one occasion, she mentioned her father had committed suicide by shooting himself and she saw the results. This must have had a profound effect on her. Although she supported me in writing Christmas cards and including letters in them, to my recollection, she never attended church. I don't even remember a conversation on the subject of God.

7

My Eyes Opened

They (older women) are to teach what is good.

—Titus 2:3

Mom wheeled me through the maroon double doors of a two-story brick building. Immediately to the left was the main office of New Britain Memorial Hospital, where Mom signed paperwork to admit me to this chronic care facility. It was midfall of my thirteenth year on earth. This was the place I would spend much of my teen and young adult life.

When the technicalities were over, we went up on an old green elevator. I had never seen an elevator open manually like a regular door. After getting off on the second floor, we went down the hall to the nurses' station where Mom signed more paperwork and discussed how to take care of me. Then we went to what was to be the first of many, many bedrooms I would share with a variety of girls and women.

As we walked into the room, a girl, probably two or three years older than me, stopped watching her soap opera. She looked at me and started rocking from side to side in her wheelchair with one hand high in the air. Sometimes when I get excited or emotional, my arms fly around, but somehow this was different. I learned later this action was a sign of her excitement, but at the moment, I was taken aback. I had never seen a person act out of the ordinary before.

The girl's name was Lynn. She had cerebral palsy like me but also had some intellectual challenges. The nurse in charge might have miscalculated the situation when matching me with Lynn. I didn't last long as her roommate. For one thing, I didn't appreciate her friend Lydia, who was able to walk, lying on my bed while visiting Lynn. It took only a month or two for the nurses to realize that the match wasn't working very well and had Lydia switch rooms with me. She had a private room, which suited me well.

From my time at New Britain Memorial Hospital, I experienced and learned much of life both in positive and negative ways. One of the profound facts that shocked and saddened me was how parents could abandon their children. Both Lynn's and Lydia's parents left them to live their entire lives in an institution. Once a year, Lynn's mom would visit her. Lynn would get so excited as the day approached, but her Mom would only stay for an hour, and then Lynn would be down in the dumps.

My first dinner was a memorable one. The food came finely chopped up and tasted like mush. Usually, I can eat regular food if the person feeding me puts the things I have to chew on the right side of my mouth near the molars. I tried to explain this to the nurse, but the message didn't get through. They didn't understand my speech yet.

A similar situation occurred with drinking. They were used to having their patients who had cerebral palsy hold their heads back while they poured liquid into their mouths. Obviously, this was a slow and difficult process for both patient and nurses' aides. As for me, I couldn't wait for Friday, which was two days away, when Mom would come to take me home for the weekend. I explained to her what was happening so she could show them how I eat and drink. So when Mom brought me back on Sunday, she demonstrated how I drink by placing a cloth firmly under my chin with one hand and, with the other, putting a cup to my mouth and gently but steadily pouring the drink into my mouth. It didn't happen overnight, but the nurse aides learned to feed and give me a drink.

The day after I arrived, I met a woman who would have a significant influence on me. Betty Cianci became my teacher, mentor, and confidante. She had a small class-room in the hospital, which had students at various grade levels and academic needs. With patience and grace, she met the needs of each of her students, eight to ten in all.

Miss Cianci, as her students called her, was probably in her late twenties or early thirties. For a time, she lived in a convent, aspiring to be a nun, but felt the Lord had called her out of that life to work with people with disabilities. She lived with her parents in the house she grew up in.

That first morning, I was glad to see my familiar typing table, which someone at Newington Children's Hospital designed for me. It had a horseshoe cutout where my torso went. I would put my elbow on the inside of the lower level where the typewriter was and lift myself up. Then the teacher would take away my wheelchair and place a regular chair under me. This enabled me to lean forward and type with my left index finger. The typewriter had a metal guard over it so I wouldn't press more than one key at a time. This may seem laborious in this age of computers, but back then, there wasn't such a thing as a personal computer. I enjoyed learning, expressing myself, and making Christmas designs on the typewriter.

I didn't always figure out Ms. Cianci's ways at first. A month or two after I arrived in her classroom, she spread out a huge piece of construction paper, taped it down to a table, and told me to handwrite the alphabet. I looked at her like she was nuts. She knew I knew the alphabet, and was also aware my fine motor skills were very limited. But out of respect for her, I started to write the ABC's. Every so often, she would repeat the exercise. Not until years later, in college and beyond, did I realize that she had been developing a way for me to highlight textbooks and put my initials on legal documents.

I started to stay for extra time after school was over. Not because I had done anything wrong, but I had found a listening ear. She helped me navigate life in that institution. There were several situations over time that became difficult to handle. One of them was with Rachel, whom I knew previously at Newington Children's Hospital. She also had cerebral palsy but had developed symptoms of pain and lack of function that wasn't typical of her disability.

Her symptoms landed her in bed for over a year. At first, I was willing to do whatever she asked. This included delivering messages to nurse aides on another floor of the hospital and rolling the head of her bed up or down to relieve pain or make her more comfortable. As time went on, her requests seemed to increase, and my patience seemed to decrease. Ms. Cianci would attentively listen while, at the same time, picking up books and other materials from the day's activities then make observations and suggestions. Some of which I readily agreed with and others I questioned, but she never steered me down the wrong path. I have a lifelong tendency to be a people pleaser, sometimes at the expense of my own best interest.

I had the privilege of receiving Ms. Cianci's teaching and informal counseling for three years. Then it was time to move on for both of us. Tears were shed when she announced she was moving to Hanover, Massachusetts, to take a new special education position. She was beloved by many, so we had a farewell party for her. But before she left, she made arrangements for a group of us to be able to attend Slater Junior High School.

8

My Mixed-Up Education

If anyone ministers, let him do it as with the
ability which God supplies, that in all things
God may be glorified through Jesus Christ.

—1 Peter 4:11

Learning is a lifelong endeavor. When you stop learning, you stop growing. Education, on the other hand, occurs primarily in the early years of life, usually in a formal setting. My education was somewhat different than the average American, who usually remembers the social aspects of school. My interaction with students other than those in segregated classrooms was very limited to nonexistent until high school.

Going to public school was, in a way, different, but in another way very similar to my past experiences. Riding and picking up several students going to two or three schools on probably one of the few lift-equipped buses in the school district was a new experience that got old quick. On the positive side, I saw and learned my way around New

Britain and learned some Spanish words, such as *que pasa* ("What's happening?) and *bueno* ("good") from Domingo. He was a chucky teenager who used a wheelchair and lived in "the projects". His aim in life seemed to be getting himself in trouble. Other words that weren't so positive or useful were also spoken.

Like most school buses, we had one or two boys who would pick on other students, some of whom were more vulnerable than others. Mind you, most of us used wheelchairs. What astonished me was that in the six years I rode that rattling bus, not one boy picked on me. There was no logical explanation for this. Somehow, they just respected me and let me be.

In 1970, it was common to have students who used wheelchairs in separate classrooms for their academic learning. This was the case at Slade Junior High School. Three grades—seventh, eighth, and ninth—were taught in one classroom by Mrs. Grace, who was a gentle, older woman with a gray prim perm. How she managed to teach three grades, take care of our physical needs, and coordinate schedules was beyond me. She only had student volunteers to help her during lunch period when they would wheel some of the students to the cafeteria, which was right next door, and then assist them in getting their meals. Some of us, like me, ate in the classroom. Looking back, it's somewhat difficult to understand. It was acceptable for some to go to music appreciation or woodworking and others not. To be honest, I suspect it had to do with physical as well as cognitive abilities. Little did I know that at that time, the winds of change were blowing, which would have a positive effect for children with disabilities for many years to come.

I entered seventh grade with four or five boys, including Domingo, all of whom had the diagnosis of Duchenne muscular dystrophy, which causes deterioration of muscles starting in early childhood. Most of us were from New Britain Memorial Hospital, but it was fun and entertaining to interact with students from town. There was Billy, a heavyset black ninth grader, who, like some kids his age, tried to act tough. He was street-smart, but motivating him to do academic work was like pulling a stubborn horse. He was the only one at that grade level, so he probably didn't receive very much academic attention. The noise of the teacher and other students was a distraction contributing to his wayward ways.

By the time I got to ninth grade, I found myself in the same position. All the boys who entered seventh grade with me had passed away. Due to their particular disability, death came early for them, usually in their mid- to late-teen years and usually in their sleep or due to a respiratory ailment. The heart, which is a muscle, just stops. Now whenever I listen to journalists mention how Americans have an aversion to the subject of death, I just shake my head. Death is part of life, and it is all around us. Nonetheless, we prefer not to face it because of the question, "Is there life after death?" or "Is this all there is?" Each person must face this question sometime in life. Circumstance determines when. I believe we will have eternal life if we recognize and accept that Jesus shed His blood on the cross to forgive each person's sins, past, present, and future. I don't know if

I'll see Domingo, Eddie, or any of the other boys in eternity because I don't know their hearts.

Unlike Billy, I loved to learn. I was up to the challenge of having Mrs. Grace spend a few minutes with me each day and take it from there, although motivating myself to read and answer questions about earth science was a little difficult. How rocks, boulders, and mountains were formed millions of years ago didn't inspire or thrill me, but I completed the assignments anyway. In my view, I taught myself ninth grade.

Entering high school was a whole different ball game. In 1975, the forerunner of the Individuals with Disabilities Education Act (IDEA), which requires school systems to give children with disabilities an education "in the least restrictive environment," was passed. Connecticut's senator Lowell Wicker was one of the champions of this legislation and for good reason. He had a child with a disability.

In anticipation of this legislation, instead of being in a segregated classroom, I was attending regular classes. Before this time, not many public schools had severely disabled students integrated into regular classrooms. So in some way, I was an experiment.

My first day was dull and boring as I spent it in the nurse's office. There was a communication mix-up, and the person who was supposed to be assisting me throughout the day was never hired by the school system. When my usually-quiet-mannered mother found out and then gave the powers that be a piece of her mind, things began to happen. The person they hired wasn't a bundle of joy, but she did her job wheeling me from class to class and assisting with my personal needs, such as feeding me lunch and taking me to the bathroom. Eventually, she somewhat understood my garbled speech, which made communication a bit easier.

I was thrilled to attend classes with all the other students at New Britain High. Going from class to class took some getting used to. The building was relatively new, so each floor was color coded with huge, bright numbers next to each classroom, but nobody told us which way the numbers progressed going up and down the halls, so we went up and down the halls repeatedly the first few days. As with any high school, there were required subjects, such as English grammar and American history.

Many memories of high school have faded, but my American history teacher stands out in my mind. She was a young, engaging woman who made history enjoyable and cared about her students. I don't think she had much, if any, experience with a person with a disability before I was wheeled into her classroom, but that didn't seem to faze her. In fact, in the spring of my freshmen year, she planned an all-day class trip to Newport, Rhode Island, to see the famous, luxurious mansions (Rockefellers, Morgans, and Breakers) built in the early 1900s. Her preparations included my needs, so she asked two football players if they would be willing to carry me on and off that bus. In today's world, no teacher would ask their students to take on this type of responsibility for safety reasons, but back then, it was a different mindset. People seemed to be more trustful of each other, less suspicious. This made us freer, both physically as well as spiritually.

On the other hand, when I selected an interior decorating class to take, I was denied without explanation. Looking back, I imagine the reason for this was that part of the classroom work was outside of the high school building and the powers that be couldn't figure out (or didn't take the time) to include me. Although I was disappointed at the time, it didn't even occur to me to make a fuss.

My second and third years went much smoother. Before the first day of school the second year, I found out they hadn't hired anyone to be my assistant. I started talking, complaining really, when one of the aides offered to take the job. It was so much easier and freeing to have someone who could interpret my speech. I was able to participate in class more effectively. My cultural anthropology teacher might not have appreciated this one day when we were discussing the big bang theory and I asked, "What created the big bang?"

A surprising day occurred in my senior year. I was sitting in a small English class that was in the library. Someone knocked at the door, and the woman instructed me to go to the office. I couldn't think of any reason anyone would need to talk to me. I didn't do anything wrong. It turned out to be good news. The guidance counselor informed me I would be inducted into the National Honor Society.

Technically speaking, I shouldn't have attended my senior year of high school. I turned twenty-two a few days before the school year started. Federal and state laws end the obligation of the state to pay for the secondary education of children. But the Education of All Handicapped Children Act (Public Law 94-142) had just been passed, and I was doing so well that a rare exception was made. Somewhere buried in a vault in the capitol building in Hartford, Connecticut, there is a document signed by Governor Ella Grasso specifically permitting me to complete my senior year. There was no fanfare or great announcement.

Mom was so proud of me both during the induction ceremony and my graduation. Each weekend during high school, she would help me with my homework. By this time, all my siblings were married, so Mom could give her attention to assisting me by reading to me, answering questions out of a workbook, or writing answers to an essay. Although I love to read, I read slowly. The induction ceremony was on a weekday evening, which meant Mom drove two hours just to watch a rope be placed on my neck, then two days later drive another two hours to bring me home for another round of homework.

Although I was embarrassed when I received a standing ovation on graduation day, Mom was pleased. I just didn't want to be singled out, to have attention on me. I accomplished what other students had. Yes, I did it with what is called a "severe" disability, which had rarely been done in that school system, but I just wanted to be part of the crowd.

9

Turbulence and a Revelation

In the world you will have tribulation;
but be of good cheer,
I have overcome the world.

—John 16:33

The late 1960s and the early 1970s was characterized by turbulence in the country. Whether watching the news with Mom or in the large dining room at New Britain Memorial Hospital, there was the drumbeat of the daily body count from the Vietnam War, racial strife, and the politics of the day that turned into Watergate.

Like many families, these events were the cause of discussions and debates around the dining room table at the Newcombe house. Both Glen and Bev were in college during that time and had contrary views from Mom, who was a staunch Republican. Mild-mannered Glen, who attended the University of Connecticut and lived at home, was forceful in his democratic-leaning views. Quiet Bev, who was away at college majority of the time, sided with

Glen and made her views known. I sat there taking it all in, not saying much, but pondering what I had heard. When it came time to register to vote in 1972, the year Connecticut changed the voting age to eighteen, I decided to register as an independent.

This was the "Age of Aquarius," as a 5th Dimensions song by "The Mama's and the Papa's" put it. It was an age of social upheaval, political strife, and questioning authority. This resulted in questioning our values and our spiritual lives.

New Britain Memorial Hospital had a pretty progressive recreation department. A small van would load people using wheelchairs who would go to the movies, rock concerts, and on occasion, the speedway. One evening, a group of us went to a local community gathering. As we entered the dimly lit room, a strange sense of curiosity mixed with caution came over me. The young people who greeted us were friendly and made every attempt to make us feel welcome. There were couches lining the walls. We sat in a circle. I don't remember what was said, but there was a long-stemmed pipe being passed around to certain persons, particularly the leaders of the group. There was a sweet smell to the smoky air. We attended the gathering two or three times, then the recreational staff stopped inviting us.

A year or two after the above event, a group of younger energetic Christians came faithfully every Wednesday evening. Marie and Cabby were the obvious leaders. Marie started every evening strumming her guitar to uplifting folk songs, which I thought she wrote. Many years later, I learned they must have been part of the new Jesus

Movement when I heard the lyrics, "It only takes a spark to get a fire going… That's how it is with God's love, once you experience it."

Cabby usually taught from the Bible in a way I never heard before. He explained things in an understandable way. I started attending the gatherings every week. One evening I was listening to his message and was struck by some things he was saying. I don't remember his exact words, but I realized Jesus died on the cross for my personal sins. I then made a decision to accept Him as my personal Savior. The full implications of this decision would only be realized by the passage of time.

That night, as I lay in bed, I contemplated on what I had just heard. All my short life, I had heard about God and Jesus who lived on the earth many years ago and taught His disciples many life lessons. But what Cabby was describing was something more, something different. He referred to this difference as the Holy Spirit. I knew something had changed inside me. I thought about these things for a few days then put them on a shelf in my mind. They would come off the shelf on Sundays, Wednesdays, and on occasion.

How many life choices would have changed if I had a mentor and grew in my faith more rapidly? The answer is unknowable.

*****

Newcombe weddings were eagerly planned throughout this period. Vaughan was the first to take the plunge into marriage in 1967 to Pauline, a Catholic girl who was meticulous. It was the first time I was in a large stone cathedral, and I was both awed and bewildered. Part of the service was in Latin, which I had no clue about.

After Vaughan graduated with a master's in certified public accounting, they settled in Tolland, Connecticut. Mom was delighted on June 9, 1972, when her first grandson was born. Named after his father and grandfather, he would eventually be known as Rick. This would be their only child as their marriage dissolved four years later.

Glen and Nancy held their wedding and reception in the backyard of our house in June of 1971. The brick patio was the perfect place to hold the ceremony. Nancy was the best as far as I was concerned. She had no problem doing things for me and treated me as a good friend. She even had me in their large wedding party. It was a shock and a heartfelt blow to me and to all the family five years later when one day she just took off for one of the Caribbean Islands, never to return to Glen. We couldn't figure out what just happened. It took a few months for Glen's heart to heal before he could explain to Mom that Nancy didn't want children. There might be other reasons unbeknownst to me, but Glen was meant to be a dad.

Bev met John Woodcock on the campus of Bowdoin College in Brunswick, Maine. John was an aspiring lawyer who had lived in Maine all his life and would entertain us with "down Maine" stories. He was the first person that I heard use the phrase "You can't get there from here" with a drawl. Of course, John had a serious side and enjoyed a good, respectful debate. Bev also held their wedding reception in the backyard of our house on a hot July day two years later. Bev had a traditional large wedding party, which primarily included family members from both sides. John was from a family of seven. The ceremony was held in Chaplin Congregational Church, where we attended services. Eventually, when John graduated from law school, Mom was blessed with three grandsons.

10

My First Love

Love bears all things, believes all things,
hopes all things, endures all things.
—1 Corinthians 13:7

I noticed him for the first time, after being home for the summer, in the large dining room of New Britain Memorial Hospital. Something instantly attracted me to him. Maybe it was the way his shoulder-length light-brown hair looked or his long oval face. Curious about the new kid on the block, so to speak, I inquired what his name was. "Kenny St. Michel" was the answer, but he was involved with Beth. That didn't prevent me from glancing his way once in a while.

Life went on. Occasionally, Kenny would say a kind word to me. I would later learn flattery and wandering eyes were part of his nature. There was a Valentine's Day party and I overheard someone read the Valentine's Day card that Kenny had given Beth. Beth was blind so was unable to read the card herself because it wasn't in braille. A pang of jealousy struck my heart. With people all around me, I had to get a grip on my emotions. I was able to stop the tears before anyone noticed. I knew I had no right to be jealous, but I was.

It was only a few months later that Kenny turned his eyes to me. I quickly learned he preferred to be called Ken. It was more manly. Besides, there was another Kenny on the same floor. There would be less confusion.

At first, we met in various locations around the hospital. Our favorite was the classroom, which was downstairs and down a long hallway. It was an out-of-the-way place where not many people frequented. Ken helped me with my Algebra homework. He wasn't too interested in math but was patient when I gave him instructions on where to put the points on a graph and where to draw the line. We would reward ourselves with kisses. The main drawback to this location was that anyone could walk into the classroom at any time. So much for privacy.

Eventually, Ken was moved into a semiprivate room with David. This enabled us to be in each other's company alone, with the door closed. We enjoyed listening to music, so we would spend hours face-to-face, our wheelchairs touching each other, as close as possible. Instead of holding each other's hands, we held each other's forearms while communicating our thoughts, dreams, and hopes to each other. In order for us to kiss, I would have to lean toward his face. His movements were restricted to some fine motor skills like writing and making model cars, which he loved to build. But oh, he knew how to kiss! In my naive experience, I was on cloud nine.

One of Ken's dreams was to be a DJ on a rock radio station. He had a clear, crisp voice, and he could identify and knew the background of most of the rock bands of the '70s. After graduating from high school, he looked into going to broadcasting school, but found roadblocks not only with the ability to obtain financial aid but also with the physical ability to manage the technical aspects of manipulating the boards that operate the radio station. In a way, this experience deflated his spirit for understandable reasons. Whenever there was a talent show at camp, he would always end up being the MC. He was in his glory in those moments.

Ken was a good-looking man, and he knew it. He used to primp in front of the mirror. There was a pop song out at the time that had the refrain, "You're so vain, I bet you think this song is about you, don't you, don't you"—"You're So Vain" by Carly Simon. Despite my speech impairment, I would tease him by singing the refrain whenever I would catch him primping.

The sexual revolution was under way, and Ken and I wanted to express our love in a physical way. We asked some younger staff whom we developed a friendship with to help us one night to go to a motel room. Naturally, fearing the consequences of being found out, they refused our request. The same thing happened when we asked family members. Although at the time this was heartbreaking, in retrospect it was God's blessing on several levels. Physically, we wouldn't have been able to do what we wanted to do. Spiritually, we would have been breaking God's law by partaking in sex outside of the bonds of marriage, although we didn't think much about that aspect. To be honest, there is a tiny little piece of me that is saddened by the knowledge Ken never had the pleasure of making love when he was on this earth.

The time came, about a year into our relationship, when he broke up with me for a new woman on staff. As any young person would tell you, the first time was the hardest. My heart was broken. Oh, those wandering eyes. In a way, I understood. She was pretty and able-bodied. He was flattered to have a nondisabled woman take an interest in him. I would see them on her break watching TV or just talking. Avoiding their eyes, I still would be interested in listening to their conversations as I passed by in the hall.

After a few months, their relationship dissolved. It took a month or two for him to lick his wounds, but he came back into my arms. This would be the pattern of our five-year relationship. One would think I would wise up, but being in love, having a forgiving heart and limited prospects makes one be accepting.

When I came back to New Britain Memorial Hospital after living at home for the summer, our reunion was poignant and somewhat prophetic. Ken was anxious for me to hear a song released over the summer by Garry Rafferty, "Right Down the Line." I was overwhelmed by the depth of meaning this song had on our relationship.

> I know how much I lean on you
> Only you can see
> The changes that I've been through
> Have left a mark on me

You've been as constant as a Northern Star
The brightest light that shines
It's been you, woman
Right down the line
I just want to say this is my way
Of tellin' you everything
I could never say before
Yeah this is my way of tellin' you
That every day I'm lovin' you so much more
'Cause you believed in me through my darkest night
Put somethin' better inside of me
You brought me into the light
Threw away all those crazy dreams
I put them all behind
And it was you, woman
Right down the line

Tears were flowing as our eyes locked together. I knew what he was saying: "Forgive me for all the hurt I've caused you, all the heartaches. You have been faithful to me." The next few months were a sweet time in our relationship.

In mid-December, when I was between waking and sleeping, I had a strange sense that Ken was in the room, which was impossible. I was in my twin bed at home. Mom was in the living room drinking her coffee, as usual. As I became fully awake, I dismissed the sensation. I had to study for my last final exam the next morning in music appreciation.

After assisting me the next morning with the music exam, Mom dropped me off at New Britain Memorial

Hospital. As was her custom, she pushed me up the steep hill from the parking lot to the door that led to the floor I was on. I would work my way to my room, pushing myself backward, while Mom went back to get my clean clothes. Mom was walking down that hallway and I was almost to my room when I saw her slip into the nurses' station, which was unusual. When Mom came into the room, she said nothing about her conversation at the nurses' station. The last thing she said to me seemed a little odd at the time but, in retrospect, was thoughtful and understanding. "If you want to come home early for Christmas, just call me."

Relieved that finals were over, I was in the hall on my way to the elevator to see my love when the head nurse intercepted me. She wheeled me back to the room, sat on my bed, and told me Ken had passed away in his sleep Saturday night while he was home for the weekend. Although this was the way for many people with muscular dystrophy, it was Ken's desire to die in a more unusual way, like a car accident.

After my initial heartfelt cry, I roamed the halls of the hospital in a semidaze. It was the evening of the annual hospital-wide Christmas party with catered food, which was always delicious, presents from Santa and a concert to top the night off, but I couldn't get into the celebration. All I could think about was Ken.

I knew I had to eat something. One of the nurses' aides, probably Bunny, fixed me a plate of food, including a lobster tail. My family grew up learning the fine art of dissecting lobsters to get every last morsel. Newcombes enjoyed their lobsters, but on that evening and for years after, lobster would have a funny taste to me. I unconsciously associated eating lobster with Ken's death and, for several years, avoided eating it. Fortunately, as time passed, so did the association, and I'm back to eating the family delicacy.

Ken was well liked, so the recreation department was kind enough to arrange for a small group of us to go to Ken's funeral. Actually, they consulted with me about whether to go to the wake or to the funeral and about who should attend. This was quite respectful considering the times and the place.

We sat in the back of the last pew in the small Catholic chapel, four wheelchairs in a row. Someone asked if I wanted to go up to the casket, but I shook my head. I didn't want to make a scene. Besides, it was an open casket, and I wanted to remember Ken as he was alive, not in death. A year earlier, I had gone to another funeral that had an open casket, which turned me off to the practice. We viewed the interment from the van as it would take several minutes to depart then get back in the van. We had an hour-and-a-half ride back to the hospital. The day did help me to process saying goodbye to Ken.

11

Preparation

For I know the thoughts that I think toward
you, says the LORD, thoughts of peace and not
of evil, to give you a future and a hope.
—Jeremiah 29:11

Like most freshmen, entering college was a whole new world for me. No more Marie to push me from class to class and assist with my daily needs. I had received my first motorized wheelchair to navigate Central Connecticut State College (now university), thanks to the Department of Rehabilitation Services.

There were several individuals who lived at New Britain Memorial Hospital who took classes there. One of them was Gary Gross, who also had cerebral palsy as well as a visual impairment. He had curly, light-brown hair and big green eyes. He wore thick black-framed glasses that seemed to perpetually look foggy. Gary was a character who didn't always think things through. He offered to show me around campus, and I readily accepted the offer.

On the day of my private tour, we were dropped off at the Administration Building, where we took care of assorted business. I was able to get familiar with that first brick building, the one with the clock adorning the roof. Then we went outside to head to the Student Center, but I quickly realized Gary was a little confused and embarrassed. Fortunately, I had a handbook that had a map of the campus on the back page. Studying the map, I located the Student Center and then located the Administration Building. The campus was relatively small, so it wasn't difficult to figure out how to get from point A to point B. But this was the first time I was totally on my own and I had Gary depending on me to get us there. We were able to cross the street without incident and enter the building safely. Once inside, Gary found his bearings and resumed his position as tour guide.

The first semester, I took two classes to get my feet wet. One of them was an introduction to psychology. The classroom was built auditorium-style with rows of approximately two hundred seats going up the stairs. This meant I sat in the very front of the classroom and every student would need to go by me. Some gave me a smile; others gave me a "What are you doing here?" look.

Like many students entering college, I wasn't sure what I wanted to major in but was leaning toward psychology. For some reason, people who lived at the hospital would come to me for advice or just a listening ear. I enjoyed helping people figure out emotional issues, but after taking two psychology courses, I decided that field wasn't for me. Learning Sigmund Freud's theory of the id, ego, and superego was too much for my brain to wrap around. Although I did well in the course, I had a difficult time swallowing the theory. The Lord must have been protecting my mind even though I didn't know it at the time.

After the first year, I decided to increase the challenge and take three courses at a time, which became my norm. Exploring various subjects was enlightening, but I settled on business administration as a major with a concentration in nonprofit organizations. Although I didn't know much about them, I figured they might be more likely to hire me than a for-profit corporation. Besides, I was drawn to the whole idea of serving people.

I soon found out that a concentration in nonprofit organizations was a challenge. The field of study was relatively new and the courses were offered on a limited basis. For example, nonprofit marketing was offered several times but always canceled at the last minute due to lack of student interest in the subject. This meant I would need to scramble to find a course to replace it. This involved waiting in line and hoping the registrar person would take the note I handed her and change the class.

My social interaction with fellow students beyond "Hi, how are you?" was limited due to my speech impairment. Although certain classroom situations were awkward, on the whole, the lack of communication didn't bother me. I'm more of a *Dead Poet Society* than an *Animal House* type, although neither one of those movies actually portrays my personality.

For fun, I found myself buying tickets to theater productions on campus. This involved some covert operations.

A short, stout man, Smitty, who drove me and others to and from classes, worked for an ambulance service. He had other pickups throughout the day and into the evening. He would offer, or I would ask him to take me places in town that were not on his schedule. One of those places was back to campus to see a play. Once or twice my roommate, Kathy, came with me. Every once in a while, for a few weeks, Smitty would disappear. We would have to get used to a new driver, and then Smitty would appear again. It became clear this was a pattern. Smitty was a likable binge alcoholic.

The way I took notes depended on the subject of the class. If it was any type of math or accounting, on the first day I would write a note to the professor requesting him or her to ask for a volunteer to take notes. Usually, there would be a volunteer who would be willing to put carbon paper in his or her notebook, which would make copies of the notes as the student wrote. Other times, I would ask the professor if I could tape-record these classes. The majority of the time, they granted permission.

I had a few classes I didn't do well in, and there were some that I would do well in until the final exam. Oh, those multiple-choice questions professors are known to trick students with.

It took seven years for me to complete college. There was a man with cerebral palsy, Roy, who was at the hospital. Although I didn't know him well, he always called me "bright one." He might have been a tad jealous of me but, at the same time, admired what I was able to accomplish. For years, he took one business course per semester. He began taking one course at a time long before I started college, and he graduated several years after me. He obtained his goal and was hired by Blue Cross and Blue Shield of Connecticut.

The Department of Rehabilitation Services paid for the majority of my tuition, so it had an interest in the next steps for my future. My counselor had arranged an "expert" to meet with me. Mom as well as Glen's second wife, Kathi, also attended the meeting, which was held in the seating area of a large multipurpose room. Shortly after meeting me and reviewing some papers in front of him, he came to the conclusion that I had faked my way through college. Shocked looks were on Kathi's and Mom's faces. The vocational counselor had a combination of an embarrassed and a puzzled look on his face. I was so insulted. Nobody knew what to say. He stood up, indicating the meeting was over, said a few pleasantries, then left with the "expert" in tow.

Graduation day was cloudy and cool with the threat of rain hanging in the air, but that didn't dampen my excitement. I had achieved my goal, with honors no less. Mom was joined by Glen and Kathi attending the ceremony. Oh, yes, there was another embarrassing moment when I received a standing ovation. This seems to have become a tradition that I have mixed emotions about. On one hand, it is worthwhile to recognize the achievement of a goal no matter who the person is. But to single out and applaud simply because the person has a disability can be embarrassing and, in a sense, demeaning. It is a matter of being equal, not special.

The night before graduation, some of my friends threw a party for me. My days at New Britain Memorial Hospital were over. It had changed. Their long-range goal was to become a rehabilitation center, which they eventually achieved, renaming it Hospital for Special Care, specializing in people with traumatic brain injuries. The start of the transition was being felt. The last year I was there, my bed was moved to five different rooms, sometimes to different floors. This meant adjusting to different aides assisting. It became abundantly clear that the administration didn't want me to come back in the fall.

I was a tad sad to leave my friends, but it was time to move on to the future.

12

Now What?

A man's heart plans his way, but
the LORD directs his steps.

—Proverbs 16:9

I t was unclear where life would take me when I permanently moved back home with Mom. She wasn't a spring
chicken, turning sixty-five in August. The plan was I would
go to the Meadows, a nursing facility, in September.

In the meantime, it was time to have fun and do a little
schoolwork. Mom had decided to hire someone my own
age to take me somewhere fun, interesting, or educational.
Fortunately, Glen must have mentioned the wife of one of
his best friends to Mom. Lisa and I hit it off immediately.
She was fun-loving, a bit weird, and a little goofy. We would
go on day trips to Caprilands Farm in Coventry, which had
locally famous herb gardens, or to the beach and gardens at
Harkness State Park. Of course, we had to see how accessible the place was. Some of the pathways at Caprilands were
accessible, but some were not; for example, the old colonial

house, which had a small tearoom and a shop, had stairs so that anyone with a mobility impairment couldn't enter.

Then there were the food/drink adventures. Lisa came from an Italian background, so she enjoyed cooking and experimenting with food. For the most part, her all-natural recipes were delicious. But every once in a while, she would go wild. Like the time she picked up this bright-pink fruit drink to take on a picnic. I was dubious because of the color, but Lisa thought it would be the greatest drink ever. After she laid out the food, we decided to start with the bright-pink drink. When both of us took our swigs, we spit it out immediately. It was horrible. Despite our one negative drink encounter, we went on to establish a tradition of celebrating our birthdays together, which are only six days apart. We continued the tradition for approximately twenty years, until life became more challenging.

We also made trips to the library on the campus of the University of Connecticut, which was in the next town. Although I had graduated, I found out in my last semester that I was two credits short of what was needed to graduate. The physical education class had been waved, but nobody explained I had to complete the two credits. The dean of the School of Business was gracious enough to let me write a paper to meet the requirements. The topic I chose was business responsibilities, which proved to be challenging due to the lack of information.

In late August or early September, Mom took me to the Meadows to be admitted. Although I previously had a tour of the facility in the spring, Mom hadn't accompanied me then. The facility was recommended by New

Britain Memorial Hospital, and a few of their patients had been transferred there. With a fresh look, I began to get a sinking feeling in the pit of my stomach. Mom did all she could to settle me into the situation. Just before she left, she leaned and quietly said, "After I come back from my trip, I'll bring you home." From this statement I knew she was uncomfortable. She would take me home every weekend until she went on her trip. She loved to travel, going to England, Scotland, and other European countries with her traveling companion, Learina Muchinger. In some ways, they were opposites. Learina was always exited and on the go, while Mom was laid-back and easygoing. Somehow their personalities complemented each other.

After Mom left, I started exploring, book in hand, and found a bright empty room that had a table to place my book on. I settled in to enjoy the story I was reading. About an hour later, I was politely but firmly asked to leave. While on the way out, I looked on the door to see if there was a sign; there was none. I was in the room for the staff. I went to my room with my tail between my legs, so to speak, and feeling like a child.

Lying in bed the next morning, I watched an aide get the woman next to me out of bed in a rough manner without even saying a word to her. The aide got her ready for the day in a matter of five minutes. It occurred to me she was being treated much like an animal. I realized I didn't even know her name. I learned she was deaf. This and other experiences would spur me on in my work in the future.

Somewhere I had heard that the Psalms were comforting, so I started reading one or two each day. Some gave me comfort. Others confused me.

There weren't many people to talk to at the Meadow. Most people who were living there had either a significant communication or cognitive disability, so meaningful conversation was limited. The majority of my day was spent reading or typing a card or letter to a friend. But unfortunately, I soon discovered some of the staff were nosey. On occasion I would find the paper or card in a different position than I'd left it. I became more careful of the content of my correspondence.

The end of October came, and true to her word, Mom brought me home. My future housing arrangements and purpose in life were still unclear. Mom and I started exploring various options.

When I met Cathy Ludlum at Camp Harkness, a camp located by the ocean in Waterford, Connecticut, which is exclusively for people with disabilities, we immediately connected. We had similar backgrounds. Both of us had lost our fathers at a young age, had spent time in Newington Children's Hospital, and even went to the same college. After camp, we started meeting for lunch every once in a while just to chat.

The chatting turned into an exploration of housing possibilities, including a shared housing arrangement similar to a group home. But the concept of group homes was starting to have negative connotations in some disability circles. They were viewed as mini-institutions designed with a particular population in mind, people who were then referred to as mentally retarded. The terminology has changed to "people with intellectual disabilities."

This was one of several reasons Cathy and I laid aside the idea. We discovered we had different needs for personal care. My needs were sporadic through the day. Because Cathy has a form of muscular dystrophy, which causes breathing issues, she needed someone around constantly. She went on to assist in developing co-op housing in Connecticut, which is a small apartment complex that members contribute to the maintenance and upkeep of the property. Throughout the years, her creative juices and advocacy skills have made Connecticut a better place to live in for people with disabilities. Most notable are advances in the areas of personal assistance services, support services, housing, and most recently, preventing assisted-suicide legislation from being passed in the State General Assembly.

Each spring came a trip. Mom was planning one of her trips to Europe with Learina. With Mom's assistance, I had arranged to go to Epcot Center, part of Disney World, with Amy, a nurses' aide from New Britain Memorial Hospital who became my friend. She was a single parent with three sons. The marriage was interracial, which, at that time, was uncommon. A number of times, Smitty had dropped me off at Amy's duplex for a few hours in the evening, and she shared some of her struggles. Her parents lived on the other side of the duplex and were supportive of her.

I was excited about the trip. At the same time, I was apprehensive because I'd never flown before. In my childhood, I was told by a doctor I could never fly because I had seizures. Although I had outgrown them, thank the Lord, there was this nagging little voice in the back of my brain telling me the doctor was correct. If I went on an airplane, I would have a seizure. Much later in life, I learned this voice was the enemy of my soul and shouldn't be listened to. We thoroughly enjoyed ourselves. We particularly liked the buildings of various countries and trying ethnic foods.

Shortly after we returned from our respective trips, Mom saw an ad in *The Chronicle*, the local newspaper, that caught her eye. It was put in by someone who was looking for a person to take care of. When we met Marie, she explained that, until recently, she was taking care of an elderly lady who passed away. Because she was a live-in companion, she needed to find a live-in situation as soon possible.

Marie and I seemed to connect with each other, although she was in her late fifties. She was an artist and would eventually paint me a still life of yellow and orange pansies. She enjoyed cooking, experimenting with tasty spices which usually turned out to be delicious dishes. Having some dietary issues, she tended toward cooking natural foods.

Marie wanted to live in the country. I was used to living in the fresh, open air, so that was all right with me. We found a small two-bedroom house in Hampton for rent. It was only two or three miles away from Glen and Kathi's house. The whole idea of setting up a house was new to me. There was a flurry of activity as Marie, Mom, and I hunted for used furniture and purchased kitchen supplies. Marie had several items she contributed to the household, including a maple table with four kitchen chairs, which eventually Marie gave to me.

Although Marie was a live-in companion, she had a day and a half off each week, from Saturday early afternoon to Sunday evening. Mom would bring me to the old homestead sometime in the afternoon on Saturday, and Mom and I would attend church the next morning. The pastor, Bob McKay, had a Cheshire cat smile and a plump body to match. Almost every Sunday, somewhere in his sermon, he would say something that would make me laugh, a little too loud or too long. It would become embarrassing. I can't always control my reactions to situations even though my brain wants to. The most memorable series of messages from Pastor Bob were from Ephesians chapter six, which describes the full armor of God that each one of us should put on daily. It would be several years later that I would grasp the meaning of the belt of truth, the breastplate of righteousness, the shoes of peace, the shield of faith, the helmet of salvation, and the sword of the spirit. For me, as with many people, faith, knowledge, and understanding grow slowly over time.

Marie found there was more personal time available to her than she had in her previous companion position. She met Richard a short time after we set up our household. Richard lived approximately ten minutes from our house. Slowly at first, then with increasing frequency, she would drive over to his house after preparing and feeding me dinner to be with him for an hour or two. It was no surprise then that one day, a year and a half later, she announced she was moving in with him. Although I was sad because I had gotten attached to Marie, there was a small part of me that was relieved. During our time living together, we had some spats, which seemed to have been increasing over time. They were mostly regarding control issues pertaining to the house. From this experience, I decided it wasn't a good idea to rely just on one person for my daily needs.

During this time, I started writing poems. The following expresses my struggles at the time:

My Mind

Hands clenched in fists,
Energy: Powerful and strong.
Energy of the mind.
Wheels are spinning
Round, round, and round
In the mind.
But the body
Does not cooperate.
The energy
It has no outlet.
Will it ever?

Acceptance

Accept me,
For what I am,
Not for what I'm not,
For my looks
May deceive you,
My manner
May disturb you.
Accept me,
For what I am,
Not for what I'm not,
I'm a simple soul,

With simple needs,
And minute wants,
And with peace
In my heart.

13

Disability Issues

And let our people learn to devote themselves
to good works, so as to help cases of
urgent need, and not be unfruitful.

—Titus 3:14

Slowly, over time, I became interested in the awareness of disability issues of a broad, governmental, systematic nature. Prior to this, my focus was on the physical aspects of the disabilities themselves.

After graduating from college and moving back home, I received a different vocational rehabilitation counselor because I was on the other side of the state. His name was Mark Jorden. Every so often, on a Saturday or Sunday, he would pop by Mom's house. Usually I was there, and he would say, "I was in the area, so I thought I would drop by."

In the general conversation, he would drop a small disability issue or suggestion. One of them was a disability magazine then called *The Disability Rag*. I subscribed to it and learned that people in wheelchairs were stopping buses in order to get legislation passed that would mandate lifts on all transportation. This was a nationwide effort organized by a group who called themselves ADAPT.

I had my eyes opened concerning many other issues, including housing accessibility and difficulties in navigating services needed by people with various disabilities, such as Social Security, Medicaid, Medicare, services for the blind, and the list goes on. The Air Carriers Act, which governs how airlines handle passengers with disabilities and their equipment, was working its way through the US Congress at the time, so there was lots of discussion about what to include in the legislation.

The Disability Rag explored some controversial issues. I was surprised one day when I saw an article regarding a mother who had cerebral palsy and needed daily assistance, not only for herself, but to take care of her baby. Her name was Leigh, and we were roommates for a little while at New Britain Memorial Hospital. The article was telling how she was advocating for support services so that she could raise her child, something very unusual, if not unprecedented. The state she was living in was bucking at funding such supports.

Mark also told me about an advocacy group that was forming. He encouraged me to attend the first meeting of a cross-disability group in Eastern Connecticut. The group was comprised of people who had various types of disabilities, and Mark and his wife, Michelle, who was a physical therapist, and Joyce Goldburg, a social worker from Norwich. We started by deciding on what our priority issues would be—transportation and housing being the two most important. We got to know each other pretty well, as we strategized together during 1986 and 1987. Chris Fine, who became our first president, came up with the name Disabilities Network of Eastern Connecticut, with input from the group. We particularly liked the word "networking" because it conjured up activity among people and ideas.

I didn't know it at the time, but there had been a movement in Connecticut and across the nation in the early and mid-1980s to obtain funding for what is now known as independent living centers. The genesis of the first independent living center was in Berkeley, California. It was established by a student named Ed Roberts, who was a quadriplegic and used a ventilator to breathe. He vehemently objected to living in the infirmary while attending the University of California. He fought to live in a dorm like the rest of his fellow students. He was bucking the system, which said he should live under medical control, known as the medical model. He graduated with a master's in political science, and in 1976 became director of California Department of Vocational Rehabilitation. In the position, he advocated successfully for state funding of the first center.

In the spring of 1987, Connecticut held its first independent living conference. Groundwork had been laid, although we didn't know it at the time, for the possibility of state funding of centers in Connecticut. Several members of our advocacy group attended the conference. It was the first time I felt welcomed in a room with a bunch of strangers. It was also the first time I saw so many people with disabilities in a noninstitutionalized setting. The hallways of the hotel were packed with people using wheelchairs, walkers, and white canes, just to name a few.

I might have caught "independent living" fever during the three-day event. It changed my thinking. Previously I would say, "I have cerebral palsy." In other words, my disability defined me. But I learned another way of viewing myself. "I'm a person with a disability (or cerebral palsy)." The difference is subtle but important. The emphasis is on the person rather than the disability. Another principle that was stressed was summed up in the word "empowerment." The concept of people with disabilities joining forces to create change as well as be responsible for their own choices was new to me. Although I was living in my own place and making my own choices, the thought of helping others to be able to do the same excited me.

State funding passed the legislature, and a request for a proposal grant was issued. Our little fledgling group applied for the grant. Several members of the group, including myself, took pieces of the request for proposal to work on. We were a little overwhelmed, to say the least. A small group would come together regularly around my dining room table to lay out pieces of paper from various individuals to assess our progress and see where we would go from there.

By this time, I had moved to a more centralized location near the University of Connecticut. It was obvious by then that I could live in my own place with individuals coming in twice a day to assist me and with a housemate who would put me to bed.

The majority of the request for proposal required us to describe the services we would provide, which were essentially the services of any independent living center. Each center is unique, considering the community in which we were a part of in Eastern Connecticut. We not only had to describe the four core services—information and referrals, peer counseling, individual and system advocacy, and independent living skills training—but also had to justify the purchase of a lift-equipped van to transport the people we worked with back and forth to our office. There was no other way for them to get there.

We obtained the grant with the assistance of what is now called the Disability Resource Center, which was one of the two existing centers at that time. Although it was on the other side of the state, it was willing to be our fiduciary.

After a flurry of activities, including hiring the executive director, Melissa Marshell, and some key personnel, the Disabilities Network of Eastern Connecticut opened in April of 1988. Melissa was an energetic young woman who recently graduated from law school. These activities weren't without some mishaps. One of them occurred after a session of interviews of key personnel. Julie Risken, who was active in organizing several groups, including ours, had given me rides in her car several times before. In order to get in a car by myself, I would hold the window frame of the car door, pull myself up, then swing my rear over to the seat. Well, on this occasion, my foot caught on something, and I went facedown on the pavement.

Melissa and Julie were able to walk but had varying degrees of balance issues due to their disabilities.

Fortunately, they were able to solicit a man to help me into the car. I felt fine, but Melissa and Julie could see I wasn't fine. There was a cut just above my right eye, which was bleeding. A trip to the ER was in order.

The three of us as well as the medical staff received an education that late afternoon. Due to my speech impairment, we decided I shouldn't be left alone. Melissa and Julie insisted that they be in the operating room with me while they put a few stitches above my eye. The ER staff couldn't figure out why we didn't have the phone number of the group home I lived in, which was nonexistent. After the procedure was over, I learned there was some hanky-panky going on in the form of kissing while I was being stitched up.

During a board of directors meeting a little shy of a year later, Melissa mentioned that the part-time position of community educator was open. The person who had previously filled the position decided to leave after a few months. That night in bed, I started praying and thinking. I thought that some of the responsibilities, like writing the newsletter, I could probably do, but there were others, like speaking in public, which I wasn't sure about.

The next morning, I called Melissa to see what she thought about the idea. She encouraged me to apply and advised I resign from the board of directors. After an interview and a short wait, I started at the Disabilities Network in late March of 1989.

It ended up that one of my favorite parts of the job was public speaking, especially when we did disability awareness presentations in schools. Cleo, my shy, unassuming personal assistant who went with me to interpret my speech, wasn't so enthusiastic. I would start by telling the students a little bit about myself and the center, have several volunteers do different activities depicting various disabilities, then opened it up to questions. There were a variety; some we heard regularly, and others were unusual. The one that stands out in my mind was asked by a high school student: "Do you think in a different language?" Umm, if I thought in a different language, how would I know how to answer the question? Of course, I didn't say that but gave a straightforward answer.

Each staff member, in one way or another, was involved in system advocacy or system change, as some called it. On a national level, many people, including Justin Dart, called the father of the Americans with Disabilities Act (ADA), were discussing with legislators and influential individuals the need for a comprehensive civil rights legislation on the federal level for persons with disabilities.

I was charged with the responsibility of arranging a meeting with US representative Sam Gejdenson. The ADA was working its way through Congress, and national disability rights leaders were encouraging local constituents to meet with their congressperson. When we met with him, most of us were surprised, even shocked, how little he knew about this major piece of legislation. While I recognized a legislator has many pieces of legislation to keep track of, it was disheartening to see his priorities were not with this bill.

On July 26, 1990, I found myself, along with approximately twenty individuals from Connecticut and two thousand from across the country, on the South Lawn of the White House for the signing ceremony of the Americans with Disabilities Act by George H. Bush. Although it was such an honor to be there, part of me felt I didn't deserve to be there. Many in the audience worked on this legislation for years, including Justin Dart and Evan Kemp. Leaders of all fifty states had been asked to select individuals in their state who had worked on advocating for this bill to be passed. Organizers of the event and the victory party that followed desired to have grassroots groups in the celebration, thus making it the largest signing to that date.

Cleo and her two daughters, Angie, age fifteen, and Jennie, age ten, wheeled me to the White House gates but weren't allowed inside the entrance because they weren't on the list of invited guests, which was expected. I became a little apprehensive but knew I would meet up with them at the victory party on the Mall, which was within walking distance of the White House. I sat at the far left of the seating arrangements but could see Justin Dart and President Bush sitting at the now famous table. Excitement was in the air. It was time for new beginnings and new possibilities.

At the end of President Bush's speech that day, he made the following statement: "The Americans with Disabilities Act presents us all with an historic opportunity. It signals the end to the unjustified segregation and exclusion of persons with disabilities from the mainstream of American life. As the Declaration of Independence has been a beacon for those all over the world seeking freedom, it is my hope that the Americans with Disabilities Act will likewise come to be a model for the choices and opportunities of future generations around the world." In a sense, he was indicating that advocating for justice wasn't over but now there was a foundation of law.

It was our first opportunity to explore the nation's capital, so after the celebrating was over, I took a few days off from work, and with Cleo and her girls, we attempted to find our way around DC. After a day or two, we conquered the nerve-racking subway system. Neither of us had any experience taking a subway until then. We finally figured out which of the different color lines went to which location. Unfortunately, I didn't have my motorized wheelchair, so Cleo pushed me everywhere in my manual chair. On one or two occasions, she had a double load when Jennie sat on my lap. We learned all kinds of things when we spent the day at the Smithsonian Institute. Another day we saw traditional historic sights. Little did I know, the next few years would find me in this city a number of times.

14

Spiritual Growth

Let perseverance finish its work so that you may
be mature and complete, not lacking anything.
—James 1:4

Growing up, my family went to a small congregational church within walking distance of our house. Our house boarded the towns of Chaplain, Mansfield, and North Windham. We walked over the little cement bridge, usually stopping for a moment to watch the Natchaug River flow downstream. It was a short walk. Mom would push my chair.

The church building was typical New England style, with a belfry steeple and plain maroon and medium blue stained glass windows. The inside had dark wooden paneling with maroon carpeting. There were four or five families who attended regularly. One of them were the Miles. All the sons had names beginning with *R*—Richard, Robert, and Raymond. The mother played the organ, and the dad was the deacon. The church wouldn't be able to function without the Miles family.

Each Sunday morning, Reverend Tom would rush in wearing his flowing back robe. He had just come from the Chaplin Congregational Church, the mother church to our church, where he had just preached the same sermon that he was about to deliver to us.

The time came when it was no longer feasible for the church to stay open because of the locations of the homes of the families who attended regularly, as most decided to attend another congregational church closer to their homes. Mom decided to try the one in Chaplin since she already had friends and connections there and it was close to our home.

A few years after our little church closed its doors, a fire broke out in the building, blackening the belfry. For several years it stood charred and forlorn. Many times, as we passed by it on our way home, there was a twinge of sadness for what once was and for what might have been.

By the late '80s, Mom and I were firmly established at Chaplin Congregational Church. Pastor Bob McKay made spiritual as well as physical changes to our congregation during his tenure. He introduced an evangelical flavor to the church, which future pastors would build on. He also was instrumental in the building of an addition and much-needed space for Sunday school classrooms—also, praise the Lord, an accessible bathroom and a ramp that complied with the building code. Mom no longer had to push me up a short forty-five-degree ramp.

When Gil Bourquin came to be our pastor in the fall of 1990, things slowly started to change spirituality for me. Even before he was voted in as pastor, I felt a connection with him, but Mom was uncertain. This was a bit unlike Mom, and looking back, it was a foretaste of what was to come. Since nobody ever approached or even thought about having me become a member of the church, I had to convince her to vote for him. In the end, I had nothing to worry about. It showed me I needed to step up and be my own person in all areas of life, not just in the disability arena.

Pastor Gil was tall in stature, had a giving spirit, and a humble heart. His wife, Linda, had long black hair and always looked well dressed. They had three daughters and a son, most of them in their teenage years.

We soon learned we had a mutual acquaintance. One day after Sunday service, he said, "Do you know Billy Robinson?" I was surprised, but I shouldn't have been. Billy was a pastor at a small church in Groton, Connecticut, but I knew him as the second president of the Disabilities Network of Eastern Connecticut. He was an amazing person who lived his life flat on his back due to his disability of muscular dystrophy, and he had a dedicated wife and two small children. He traveled around on a gurney and used an early version of a voice-activated computer program. He had a gifted way with words. When testifying before a committee of the Connecticut General Assembly, it was effective as legislators perked up and listened when he spoke.

One of the giftings of Pastor Gil was connecting the Old and New Testaments and bringing them to life. Before he came, I didn't realize Jesus is present throughout the Bible, being referred to by many different names.

He explained Old Testament characters in an understandable way and with background and insight. For example, when Moses heard the voice from the burning bush, several scholars believe it was the voice of Jesus, the Son of God.

He also brought the gift of praise and worship music to our little country town, and many thought it was refreshing, others not so much. Most of his family was musically talented and would help lead worship with a mixture of hymns and the more modern praise and worship music. As time went on, Pastor Gil shared some of the songs he had written, most of which were taken from the Scriptures.

On one Sunday a few years after Pastor Gil had arrived, he made an announcement that the church was looking for volunteers to be on the church committee, which was an elected position. At that moment, I didn't think much of the announcement, but over the next few days, it kept popping in my head. I had a desire to step up and serve the Lord but was unsure of myself and how the idea would be received. After some prayer, I met with my friend Sara Sabo, who was very active in the church. She knew the lay of the land, so to speak, and gave advice as to whether or not I should put my name in the hat. Encourager as she is, she told me to go for it.

It came as a bit of a shock to me when at the first committee meeting, I was selected to be secretary. By this time, I had enough experience in my job to be familiar with the duties involved in being a secretary. The committee agreed I could tape-record the meetings in order to take minutes. It took time, but thanks to the computer, I developed shortcuts.

In late April, during a meeting, Pastor Gil said he would be away one Sunday in May to be on a retreat. Then he said, "You are all invited to come." But he was looking directly at me, or so it seemed. I was going through a difficult emotional time. Mom's memory had been declining for several years, and it was at the point where the family was considering putting her in a nursing facility. He was going through a similar situation with his father. On two or three occasions he and I compared experiences and looked to the Bible for answers. He quoted from Revelations 3:20, "Behold, I stand at the door and knock. If anyone hears my voice and opens the door, I will come in to him and eat with him, and he with me." He explained that Jesus was knocking at the door of my heart, and through prayer and spending time reading the Bible, He would answer my questions.

After the meeting, I inquired about the retreat. Pastor Gil told me when it was, and he would give me the application the next Sunday. I had assumed I could take someone with me to assist me in my activities of daily living. When I found out I couldn't, I started to wonder what I was getting into. He tried to assure me there would be plenty of nurses to assist me, but this wasn't much of a comfort. I had found out from experience that many nurses and other medical professionals have preconceived notions or techniques that don't always work on specific individuals.

A week before the retreat, I got a call from a woman named Brenda, who explained she had been a Licensed Practical Nurse (LPN) for over twenty years, and she had a daughter-in-law who had a spinal cord injury. She would be one of the ones assisting me. The call did calm my nerves a little, but I was still apprehensive. It turned out she planned who would assist me the entire weekend.

Pastor Gil and I arrived at Cathedral Camp in East Freetown, Massachusetts, on a warm, sunny spring evening. As we got out of the van, we saw that the place where the retreat was being held was part of a convent, which seemed a little odd. I later came to understand the retreat I was participating in was a small part of an international ecumenical movement called Tres Dias, which means "three days" in Spanish.

I hit the panic button again later that evening when the leader of the weekend, Lynn Crème, announced a period of silence for self-reflection and to prepare our hearts for whatever God had for us. But for me, I was wondering how I was going to communicate with the women assisting me. I had written a note explaining my routine, but there were surely unexpected things that would come up. It was a relief when we arrived in the bedroom and Brenda explained, in a whisper, that an exception was being made. We would be allowed to communicate when I was getting ready for bed and also in the morning. I was grateful for God's grace in this matter, but this was only the beginning of the provisions He had made for that weekend.

The majority of time during the three days was spent in small groups listening to and discussing talks given by women plus Pastor Gil. Friday morning was spent getting to know one another and coming up with a name for our table. My computer had been set up to assist me in communicating, but, by the time midafternoon came, the computer was packed away. Between the four others around the table, they could understand my speech faster than I could type, even with a word prediction program.

The weekend was engulfed in God's love. As the three days progressed, our little group started to open up and share some painful experiences. The woman who sat to my right, who liked to play pranks and do silly little things, shared how, as she was growing up, her mother repeatedly abused her. Her mother would slam her against the wall and she was starting to do the same thing to her little girl. This was one of my first encounters with domestic violence in an up close and personal way involving a mother-daughter relationship. Because it didn't remotely come close to the relationship I had with my mother, I was at a loss for words, but the Holy Spirit wasn't.

As the conversation progressed over the next three days, emotional healing occurred among us. At one point during the weekend, both of the other two women who had never experienced Tres Dias before attempted to leave but were prevented from doing so for various reasons. I also shared the profound pain of slowly losing the essence of my mother to diminishing memory and facing the reality that she would end up in a nursing home.

Throughout the weekend, each table gave a synopsis of what we had gleaned from the fourteen talks to the others gathered. During the closing ceremony, each table was asked to present one synopsis selected by the leaders. The topic that was selected for my table to present was "action." Our table had concluded that prayer was an action, which was a revelation to some of us. We also pointed out that anyone can pray.

During our two-hour drive back home, Pastor Gil gave me some suggestions and vaguely hinted at the future. He told me, "John and Sara Sabo would be a great asset to Tres Dias. If I'm not around, can you make sure they both go on a weekend?" This became my first Tres Dias assignment, but it took several years and some persistence to see it to its fruition.

I have had the honor of remaining involved in this ecumenical movement to build leaders for the church of Jesus Christ. Leaders of six separate weekends have called Cleo Pearl and I to serve "on team," as it's referred to, usually in the capacity of prayer angels. It has also been for me a joy to sponsor several women to attend a weekend, including Sara and Cleo. Each woman has her own experiences and takeaways from the three days.

15

Memory

Even though I walk through the valley
of the shadow of death,
I will fear no evil, for you are with me.
— Psalm 23:4a

One's identity and sense of place rely on our memories. My family had slowly realized this reality over a period of many years.

Shortly after Mom turned seventy, she felt something was not quite right, so she went to the doctor. She had not been to a doctor in fifteen years. She was always healthy, making the saying "An apple a day keeps the doctor away" true. She was told she had a clean bill of health. We put the incident out of our minds.

A few years later, she went up to Hancock Maine, a place familiar to my family as Bev's in-laws owned a summer cottage there. It's a beautiful spot overlooking the water. If you look far to the right, you can see Mount Desert Island, home of Acadia National Park and Bar Harbor. In her traveling days, Mom had taken me up there to visit Bev and her two young sons, Jack and Patrick. Her third son, Chris, wasn't born yet. But Mom seemed reluctant to go on trips anymore.

When Glen and Kathi were about to leave for home, Mom couldn't find her watch, which my dad had given her. It was precious to her. Although Bev reassured Mom that she would look for it after they left, Mom talked about it most of the way home, which was unlike her. This was one of the first memory challenge incidents of many that increased over time.

Mom slowly restricted her social activities. She stopped going to the Garden Club and Philanthropic Educational Organization (P.E.O.) meetings, a Christian organization concerned with education. We were beginning to be concerned about her. To give her companionship, my two bothers did some research and decided to purchase a Yorkshire terrier for her. For many years, Mom had cats around the house, not dogs. Misty, who was her feline friend for twelve or more years, had gone to see her Maker just a year or so before. When I first met Cookie, the name Mom decided to give the dog, I mentally scratched my head and said to myself, "What were they thinking?"

Cookie was a lively little creature who loved to nip at anything that moved, whether it be a mop when Cleo was trying to clean her kitchen floor, a string, or my feet. He would jump up and down and nip with delight. But sometimes Mom wasn't so delighted and Cookie would end up in the laundry room with the door closed. She had difficulties disciplining him at times. She had a love/dislike relationship with him. Cookie lasted a year and a half with Mom then went to live with Glen and Kathi. He had a short life. Due to his hyperactivity, he had a stroke and passed away.

We started to notice little things. Sour milk in the refrigerator. Unpaid bills. A decrease in interest in the things she did the most, such as reading, gardening, and chatting with old friends. One afternoon while driving me back to the condo, she told me she thought Vaughan was stealing her money. "Why do you say that?" I replied, knowing full well he would never do such a thing. "He went in my desk," she said accusingly. I didn't know how to respond. This was so unlike Mom.

Phone calls started to increase as she became unsure of herself. If she was supposed to pick me up on a Saturday afternoon for my usual overnight stay, she would call in the morning to see what time to pick me up even though she had been getting me at the same time for years. Then two hours later, she would call with the same question. Her calls increased in frequency over time. Sometimes our conversations were a repeat of one a few days ago. When it got to the point when sometimes the phone would ring fifteen minutes after I hung up, my frustration level increased.

Sometimes it takes me a while to learn some things. Many of us are dense when it comes to certain issues like being accurate. I would find myself correcting Mom when she was telling a story, usually on dates or places. On occasion, I would get irritated looks, but most of the time she wouldn't say anything. It took a while before it dawned on me—I was hurting Mom by correcting her. She couldn't retrieve the correct information from her brain. *Lord, forgive me for my stubborn and foolish ways.*

I began noticing that it was more difficult for Mom to get me up the two steps in the garage into the kitchen. There was also a step between the kitchen and dining room, which was tricky in the best of circumstances because of the small space. She would need to tilt my wheelchair up, place the front wheels on the step, then lift the back of the chair and push at the same time. She did this for decades, but now it was physically straining her, although she probably wouldn't have admitted it.

After praying and thinking about the situation, I called Glen. One of the many gifts he has is a calm demeanor and the ability to see all angles of a situation. He can see a solution and present it in such a way that would make all feel positive about the solution. This occurred in Mom's familiar living room, Mom sitting in her favorite place on the medium-blue couch and Glen sitting in the upholstered chair, which matched the curtains. She sat listening as he presented the situation and told her I would be hiring two people who would alternate every other Saturday evening and Sunday morning. She could meet me at church, which pleased her. The conversation went better than I thought it would. In a way, Mom might have been relieved, although she didn't say anything to that effect.

Vaughan and Glen accompanied Mom to her doctor to find out what was going on with her. After some tests, the diagnosis was positive—dementia. Potentially, it could be Alzheimer's, but the doctor explained that diagnosis couldn't be established until after death. In the years to come, several of Mom's siblings, particularly her sisters, would be diagnosed with the same condition. There is now growing evidence that there are several different types of Alzheimer's disease, including a genetic type. But in the early to midnineties, information and research were just emerging. It was Nancy Reagan who assisted the process, along with writing her book, where she described her experiences with her husband, President Ronald Reagan, who was diagnosed with the condition a few years after leaving office.

Like millions of others, my family had started down a difficult road. At times it would be a little bumpy, but with faith and love, we made it through. It was particularly hard on Bev, far away in Maine. Usually when she came down for a visit, she would see significant changes while those of us who saw Mom weekly got used to the changes.

One year, after a delicious Thanksgiving dinner and when the cleanup in the kitchen was completed, as was the custom, the family gathered in the living room for a chat and some, mostly young males, around the television in my bedroom to watch the football game. We were catching up on family news when suddenly Mom started describing about my birth. Most of us had heard the story before, how she sent my dad home because it was getting late and he needed to be there for the children, how she was left alone in a room for a while when she was about to give birth, how I was born feetfirst instead of headfirst and had to be rushed to Hartford Hospital. But the story had a new word in it. She said it was a "tragedy." There was a second of silence, then the conversation continued to a different topic, but I was taken aback.

Part of me knew Mom didn't really mean I was a tragedy; she had showed me love and cared for me all my life. It was her condition that placed this negative word in her. The human brain is the most complex organism on this planet, and sometimes over a lifetime, signals get crossed. Plaques were forming in her brain, preventing the correct signals from being connected. And yet, even knowing this, the thought occurred to me, "Did Mom really think my life was a tragedy?"

Mom started mentioning moving to senior housing in Mansfield, which was a surprise. None of us could think of her living anywhere else, but she was getting older. It might have been her way of preparing for the future, but nothing came of it. She knew something wasn't quite right, but she didn't talk about it. She continued to take walks up on the hill behind her house and talk to the birds. They would sometimes sing back to her. Her favorite time each day was when the sun was setting behind the hill and the sky would turn various shades of red, blue, purple, and pink. Each day was a different delight of colors.

As usual, I went to church one Sunday morning fully expecting to see Mom there. The service started, but there was no Mom. My assistant and I exchanged worried looks. I sat through the service but couldn't concentrate on what Pastor Gil was saying. He came to me immediately after the service was over and inquired about Mom. After a short prayer with him, my assistant and I headed over to Mom's house. She wasn't there either. Half an hour later, Pastor Gil and a frazzled and confused Mom arrived. By this time, Vaughan and Glen had been called and were on their way to take care of the situation.

It was time to convince Mom to have someone move in with her. My brothers found a quiet middle-age woman who would stay at the house during the week. It so happened my two assistants who alternated working for me every other Saturday evening and Sunday mornings needed extra money, so they would stay with Mom Saturday mornings and sometimes on Sunday afternoons. For two years, Vaughan and Glen alternated weekends filling in the hours that weren't covered, including staying overnight on Saturdays. Since Glen had to be with Mom every other Sunday until after dinner and I needed assistance, he and Kathi decided to hit three birds with one stone and brought their two children and Mom to my condo to eat. Kathi was an awesome cook, so we always had delicious healthy meals from her kitchen. More important, we had family time, where Geoff and Marj got glimpses of their Nana's and aunt's lives.

The day came when during a conversation on the brick patio outside the back door of her home, Mom was having difficulty understanding my speech. The one person who almost always knew what I was saying, didn't. At that moment, I realized dementia would have a profound effect on Mom and the whole family. That night, lying in bed, I let myself feel a deep sadness. The relationship with Mom had changed and would change further over time. This was the time prayers began to be sent from my bed. *Lord, be with Mom. If it's your will, heal her or take her to be with You.*

Every few months, we would notice that there had been a decline in Mom's cognitive ability. She began not to remember the names of people she had known for years.

We decided to place her in adult day care, a program managed by a nursing facility near Mom's home. This relieved the woman living with her. Mom couldn't be left alone anymore. She wandered at night.

Then the crisis came. A day care worker found a bruise on Mom's arm, an indicator of abuse. Bev came down to take care of her for a short time, and we had a family meeting to decide where to go from here. The answer was obvious, but my heart wasn't ready. It probably never would be ready to place Mom in a nursing facility, but there was no other option. Part of the advocacy work at the Disabilities Network was to get people out of nursing facilities or prevent them from going into them in the first place. It was also a reminder of my past experiences.

Vaughan and Glen found a small facility in Plainfield, Connecticut, approximately forty-five minutes from where I lived. Each Monday evening for the first five years Mom was there, I visited her there. Of course, the first time was the hardest. She had been admitted earlier that hot July day, so everything was new to her, as it was to my assistant and me. We pulled up to the front door of the brick building and became bewildered. All we could see were steps. The assistant who was with me went in to investigate the situation. There was a cement ramp in the back of the building, which appeared to be at a forty-five-degree slope. I thought, "How do they get patients who use wheelchairs in and out of here?" and was grateful for my motorized chair, which could make it easily up the steep incline.

I found Mom sitting in a chair in the hallway. She perked up when she heard my voice. A nurse directed us to

Mom's room and guided her to sit on her gold upholstered chair that she sat on to watch TV in days gone by. The room was arranged with several familiar objects from her home. In addition to her gold chair and her dresser, there were several pictures to make it homey. The large black-and-white painting of two snowy owls that hung in her living room now was placed on the wall near the window. Above the bed was a photograph of Bev on her wedding day throwing her bouquet of flowers. On the dresser was a picture of Dad and younger versions of Vaughan, Glen, and me.

We explored the room a little, opening up the closet and dresser drawers to familiarize ourselves with the contents. My brothers and I had agreed to wash Mom's laundry, alternating among the three of us. I found it ironic I would be helping wash her laundry. For many years she transported my laundry back and forth to Newington Children's Hospital and New Britain Memorial Hospital.

When we were ready to leave, after saying goodbye, Mom started to follow us. One of the nurses' aides saw this happening and tried to detour her. She was determined to follow us. Down the hall she went, straight to the back door. There was a combination code to open the door, which someone had to show us how to operate. I was struggling to hold back tears. The reality of seeing Mom in the nursing facility, knowing she would probably spend the rest of her life there and memories of being in an institution flooded my soul. Down the ramp, across the pavement, and into the van I went as quickly as possible. After the van started,

I hit the cassette to go into the player. "Majesty, worship His majesty…" We rode in silence most of the way home.

This was when I started to pray, "Lord, protect Mom, and if it's her time, have her come to You quickly." It would be nine and a half years until this prayer was fully realized.

In the meantime, each Monday we would make the trek to Villa Maria to bring Mom a treat; homemade apple-sauce and fresh raspberries, blueberries, or peaches were her favorite. Lotion was put on her hands and I usually got a smile or some words. In the first few years, Mom liked to "push" me up and down the hall. Actuality, she wasn't pushing me but holding on to the handles on the back of my motorized wheelchair. It was natural for her to think so; she had been pushing a wheelchair for over thirty-five years. She enjoyed our little walks until I took a turn she didn't want to take, and she made her displeasure known. Depending on who was with me, we would sing hymns to her, which usually got a smile or even a couple of words.

As her recognition and responses decreased, so did the length of time between visits. It happened slowly. I would miss one week every once in a while. Then it became two. Part of me felt guilty, but it was difficult to see her just sit-ting or lying there. Mom wasn't Mom anymore.

The inevitable phone call came on New Year's Eve morn-ing, made by Glen, who informed me of her passing in the wee hours. By this time, I had left Chaplin Congregational Church and asked Pastor Kevin White to preside over the memorial service. Mom was with Jesus, beyond the sunset now, but her memory on earth will live on.

16

New Creation

Therefore, if anyone is in Christ, he is a
new creation; old things have passed away;
behold, all things have become new.

—2 Corinthians 5:17

"There was someone who worked at Eden this summer. I heard she was looking for work, can't remember her name. Her mother is Nancy Goodrich," my friend Sara said in her always-willing-to-see-possibilities voice.

"Michelle leaves in a few weeks for her vacation. I need to find someone before she leaves," I replied.

Michelle was an Eastern student whom I had hired in early September as a personal assistant to work some evenings and every other weekend.

"I know," Sara said reassuringly. "I'll make a call and see if she's interested."

"Thank you."

"Yep." I hit the button to hang up the phone.

Sara knew numerous people in the community between her leadership at Chaplin Church and her position as manager of Interim Health Care, a home health care agency. On more than one occasion, her connections had helped me find personal assistants. A very enthusiastic, musically talented person, she led the small choir in our church.

That night I prayed again, "Lord, send me someone to assist me while Michelle is away. You have someone picked out. Send her to me."

A few days later, I arrived home from work and noticed there was a message on the answering machine. Hitting the button, I heard a chipper voice saying, "Hi, my name is Pam. Sara Sabo called me and said you were looking for someone to help you for a few weeks. I'm interested in the job. You can call me at—" And she left her number.

Pam took long strides as she entered the living room of my condo. "Hi, nice to meet you. I've heard about you from Mom," she said.

I gestured with my arm for her to have a seat on the chair on the right side of the table. I wheeled my motorized chair to the end of the table.

"You can take your coat off," Cleo said. Pam quickly jumped up, took her coat off, placing it on the back of the wooden dining room chair, then sat back down. She wore black jeans, a black sweatshirt with a western scene on the front of it, and work boots. She had reddish-blond hair that was a few inches past her shoulders. Her face was dotted with freckles, but the lines near her eyes and mouth indicated a hard life.

"I'm Cleo, Carolyn's personal assistant."

I added, "She has been working for me for over ten years."

Cleo repeated what I said.

"That is why she can understand me so well."

Cleo again repeated the sentence for Pam.

"Anyway, first I'll ask you a few questions, then tell you a little about the job. First, tell me a little about yourself."

"Well, as you know, I worked at Eden this summer. I enjoyed working with autistic children. I've also worked at some group homes and at UCP (United Cerebral Palsy) in Hartford. Right now, I work at Rite Aide, you know, the pharmacy next to Big Y. I'm living with my mom right now. I have two grown children. That's it."

"Do you like to cook?"

"Yes, Mom and I do a lot of cooking."

"Are your hours flexible?" Cleo was repeating every question for Pam. We knew she wouldn't understand my slurred speech.

"I work at Rite Aid until four, but I could be at your house at four thirty."

"Sometimes I have meetings at night. They go until nine or ten, sometimes later."

"No problem."

"Do you like to drive?"

"I love to."

"Sometimes I have meetings in different parts of the state, such as Groton or Hartford."

"That's fine."

"The blue van outside is mine," I explained, with Cleo repeating.

Cleo took over the explanation of the van. "It has a ramp that comes down. She wheels herself in and you buckle the wheelchair down."

"Yes, I've driven vans before."

"Do you know what my disability is?"

"Cerebral palsy."

"Of course, you know that. You worked for UCP, but do you know what it is? I'll give you a brief explanation anyway. That way we will be on the same page. CP is a neurological condition that is caused by a lack of oxygen at birth. It affects the part of the brain that controls your movement. I don't have complete control over my movements. As you know, every individual with CP is different. Don't worry about understanding me, it takes time."

"I'm getting a few words already."

"I have a hard time understanding her sometimes. She has to spell out words for me sometimes," Cleo added.

"I have a letter board around here somewhere. I hardly ever use it. I can point to letters to spell on it. It's probably buried in the closet. Anyway," I said, changing the subject, "what do you think are qualities you need in this job?"

Pam looked puzzled for a second, then replied, "Patience, caring, reliable."

"Oh my," I thought, "someone who actually used the magic word." So many times, interviewees will assume I'm looking for the words "patient" and "caring," but I'm really looking for "reliable" and "responsible." If someone doesn't show up when they're supposed to, I might not eat dinner or get up in the morning until I find someone to rescue me.

"We'll go over what the job is. You would be working weekday evenings and every other weekend." Pam nodded in agreement as if to say this is what I understood. "On Mondays, Wednesday, and sometimes Fridays you will pick me up from work. This means picking the van up at four thirty and driving down to Disabilities Network of Eastern Connecticut (DNEC).

"You would pick me up. Bring me home, cook, and feed me dinner and take me to the bathroom. Mondays, Wednesdays and sometimes Fridays you will pick me up from work. Tuesdays and Thursdays I will meet you here at 5:00. This may change from week to week. As I said, I have meetings for work. On Mondays, I usually go see my mother. She's in a nursing home in Plainfield. She has Alzheimer's disease. Do you have any questions?"

"Not that I can think of right now."

"I'll call you in a day or two."

Pam swiftly got up and put her coat on. "It was nice to meet you."

As she walked to the door, I thought to myself, "She doesn't have much competition." Wrong time of the year and only four weeks. But I have a policy of not telling a job candidate that she has the job at the end of the interview. I like to leave my options open. But in this case, there were no other options. God was saying, "Hire Pam."

When spring came, Pam was still working for me. Michelle's schedule had changed, so she had to cut the hours she worked for me. Pam was glad to increase her time. I was in a dilemma. It was the first Easter Mom was in Villa Maria. I was uncertain what to do about Easter dinner, so I asked Pam if she would like to go out to eat. Since her mom was taking her extended annual vacation in Florida, she was delighted to accept the invitation. We selected Mansfield Family Restaurant, which was five miles from my condo.

After perusing the menu and selecting from an array of delicious choices the dish each wanted to try, I attempted to start a conversation. "So, did you usually eat Easter dinner with your mom?"

"When I lived with Dennis, I didn't see Mom much," she replied.

"How long did you live with him?"

"About five years," she replied as she gave me a bite of salad. I pondered this for a few seconds. "We lived in Manchester in a second-floor apartment. I fell down the stairs one time," she continued. "I must have had one too many beers that icy night. The place was a dump."

I was a little puzzled, so I started questions but didn't want to seem noisy. "You lived with Dennis before you moved back to your Mom's?"

"Yes, that was about six months ago. Poor mom, sometimes she didn't know where I was for weeks and she would worry."

I wanted to ask her why she wouldn't talk to her mother for weeks at a time, but somehow thought it was inappropriate. I couldn't have imagined not talking to my mom for any great length of time before her capacity became limited. On the other hand, I wasn't that naive to think all mothers get along with their daughters; personalities clash, misunderstandings occur, and rifts develop. But it was difficult to imagine this occurring with Pam's mom, Nancy, who was a sweet, energetic lady in her early seventies.

"You were married at one time, right?" I inquired. I saw what could be our entrées being delivered. Pam followed my eyes and greeted the waitress with a smile. We rearranged the table and indulged in our first bits of seafood and lamb.

"Oh, yeah, you did ask about my marriage. Well, I started dating my ex-husband when we were in high school. I was fifteen and thought I knew it all. We got married two years later, and I had my daughter shortly after, my son came five years later."

"Did you work?" I asked.

"Oh, yes, we both worked for the Post Office. I worked for them for ten years delivering the mail. It was a family affair." She gave me bites of the delicious seafood casserole as she kept on talking.

"So, what happened?" I knew I was getting personal, but she had the option of telling me just as much as she wanted me to hear.

"Well, he started verbally abusing me shortly after we got married. At first it was just occasionally. I didn't like it, but no big deal. We partied every weekend, from Friday night to Sunday. First it was only beer and occasionally weed. You know, marijuana was everywhere back then."

I nodded my head in agreement, remembering friends smoking in my presence and inhaling the heavy, pungent smoke. The smoke from marijuana was never enough to get me high. I didn't have the ability to suck, so I couldn't smoke. Many moons ago, getting high mildly fascinated me, but I came to realize God doesn't want anyone to be under the influence of a substance that prevents them from knowing him.

"The swearing gradually increased, and one day when my son was young, my ex-husband hit me." A hint of anger was in her voice as Pam continued, "I left him and the kids. I promised myself before I married that I wouldn't put up with a husband who was abusive." Then tears welled up in her eyes. "My son won't talk to me now. He blames me for everything, for leaving. He won't even talk to his grandmother." Tears were streaming down her face. "I made a mess of my life." She dabbed her eyes with the napkin, trying to regain her composure.

I didn't quite know what to say. I knew Pam had heard about Jesus. In fact, she just started meeting with the new pastor weekly, but obviously, the love and forgiveness of Jesus didn't penetrate her soul yet.

"I got odd jobs and eventually began living with Dennis. I didn't want my mom to see where I was living, so I wouldn't contact her." Tears filled her eyes again. "She found out where I lived and came to see me." She laughed a little and added, "She, with the help of Dick, staked me out. They would sit and wait for me until I came home from work or from wherever I was. After a while, Dennis and I didn't get along, so I moved in with Mom about six months ago." She had regained her composure and was smiling a little.

The waitress came to clear away and wrap our plates. "Dessert?" she asked.

We exchanged glances and decided to share a sweet.

That night while lying in bed, reviewing the conversation I had with Pam, I prayed to the Lord to give me the words to minister to her heart.

One steamy summer evening, Pam and I sat in the van waiting for Michelle. We were silent for a few minutes, watching the sun set and reflecting on life. I broke the silence with the request, "Can you open the window? It is getting hot in here." Pam leaned across my lap and rolled down the window.

"Did you ever wonder what the future holds?" Pam asked out of the blue.

"Yes, many times," I replied, then almost as an afterthought, added, "The Lord has a plan for you."

She turned to me with a surprised look on her face, as if to say, "What are you talking about?"

"I believe I was meant to be the director of DNEC." I continued, "looking back, there were many experiences which led me to the position I have today."

"But how do you know what the plan is?" Pam questioned.

"You don't always know. Sometimes you know, but many times you don't, not until years later," I replied. "I was in a nursing home for a short time. The first morning I was there, I saw an aide come in with a wheelchair, yank the lady next to me out of the bed without speaking a word to her, and bring her to the bathroom. Within five minutes, the aide had the lady dressed."

"That's not right. You don't treat people like that." Pam's voice was a mixture of irritation and dismay.

"Exactly, that's why I have a passion to get people out of nursing homes. At DNEC, we advocate with persons in nursing homes to get them out and living in the community." I thought she might understand the general concept but would have no idea of the details involved in getting a person out of a nursing facility.

We sat quietly for a few minutes then Pam looked straight into my eyes and inquired, "Do you really think God has a plan for me?"

I just nodded and affirmed, "Yes, He does," but thought to myself, "But you need to surrender first to Jesus."

It was almost dark. Finally, Michelle came out of her girlfriend's apartment, so we could go home.

A week or two later, Pam was feeding me dinner at the dining room table when the phone rang. Pam answered it. From what I gathered from overhearing her side of the conversation, it was Pastor Sonny, the new pastor of Chaplin Congregational Church. A month or two ago, Pam had started to meet with him weekly so he could counsel her in her search for faith and truth. Apparently, she had left him a message asking his advice on whether or not to go to an Alcoholics Anonymous meeting that night. Understandably, he advised her not to attend any AA meeting because the organization promotes relying on a vague "Higher Power" instead of the atoning and forgiving grace of Jesus.

While I understood Pastor Sonny's reasoning, I had a different perspective. A believer in peer mentoring, I had seen the power of one person with a disability mentoring another person with a similar disability. Essentially, this is what Alcoholics Anonymous is, a peer support group. Although AA had originally been established on Christian principles, it had drifted away from those values. I didn't know it at the time, but there is a Christian-based group which is quite similar to AA, called Celebrate Recovery.

As Pam hung up the phone, I saw a questioning and confused look on her face.

"I don't understand why he doesn't want me to go to an AA meeting," Pam said irritably.

"Well, he probably wants you to rely on Jesus to help you through things," I replied.

"But when I read the Bible, I don't always understand it," Pam complained.

"Some parts of the Bible are harder to understand than others." I saw in her eyes a deep desire to change, even a desire to know Jesus, but she didn't know how.

That night as Pam was about to turn out the light after putting me to bed, I ended the night with "I'll pray for you. You need a Christian friend." I learned much later that she went out that night and had a number of beers, but these statements stuck with her. She mulled them over in her mind.

As I lay praying and thinking, it occurred to me it might be time to arrange for Sara and Pam to have a time of prayer.

We arrived at Sara's house after a short visit with Mom. Sara's husband, John, greeted us outside the house, automatically got my manual chair out of the back of the van and comfortably transferred me from my motorized chair to the manual one. He was used to the routine of getting me up the steps.

Once inside the house, John disappeared. The house was full of people, as usual, mostly teenagers. John and Sara had four children in their late teens and early twenties. They had always created a welcoming atmosphere and had taken in individuals in need of a helping hand and mentoring in the Lord.

After a few pleasantries, Sara suggested, "Oh, why don't we go on the deck, it's quieter out there. I can get you out there, no problem." She opened the slider and eyeballed the step. "Oh, yes, we can do this," she said as she moved some furniture out of the way. I was a bit dubious but went along with her excitement. Pam got in front of me to hold and guide the wheelchair while Sara tipped it back on its back wheels to bump it down the step. Sara underestimated the steepness, and to our surprise, the back of the chair landed on the deck with my feet in the air.

After the peals of laughter were over, Sara got my chair in an upright position. "Oh, I need to go get the oil," Sara said, regaining her composure. Pam looked a little surprised but didn't say anything.

Quickly coming back, Sara placed a small glass bottle on a nearby table and began the conversation by asking gently but seriously, "How are you?"

Pam knew this wasn't a casual inquiry. "I don't know how I'm doing."

"You are living with your mom. How is that going?" Sara questioned.

"Poor Mom, I worry her. I enjoy living with her, but she wants to know where I am all the time. She gets nervous when I don't come home on time. In a way, I understand. I have left her not knowing where I was so many times, but I'm not a child. Oh, I made a mess of my life."

"Do you want your life to change?" Sara asked.

"Yes," Pam replied, "but I don't know how. I like meeting with Pastor Sonny, and he teaches me from the Bible, but…" Her voice trailed off.

"What you learn doesn't stay with you?" Sara questioned.

"I'm a failure. I can't do anything right." Pam started to sob. Sara gave her a long embrace.

Sara gently released her as the sobbing subsided. "My son won't even see his grandmother, never mind me, and my daughter barely speaks to me," Pam exclaimed through her tears.

"Would it be okay if we pray with you?" Sara asked. Pam nodded in assent.

"Have you ever been anointed with oil?" Sara inquired.

"No," came the reply with a questioning tone.

"The Bible instructs us to anoint people who need healing. It seems like your soul needs emotional and spiritual healing." We bowed our heads and our hearts as Sara began, "Oh, Father God, glory to your name. We lift Pam up to you right now. We thank you for Pam's life. You know all of Pam's hurts and sorrows. You have seen what she has been through throughout the years, although she may not have felt your presence."

Pam started sobbing.

"Release your healing power. Wrap your loving arms around her. May she know Jesus has forgiven all of those who believe in Him and who turn away from their sins."

The sobs were uncontrollable. The concept that God would forgive her for the unspoken things she had done to her son and daughter, her mother, and others was overwhelming. Sara silently held her close for a white.

That night as I lay in bed, I renewed my prayers for surrender and salvation for Pam. *Oh, Sovereign Lord, you know all things. You know Pam's heart. Lord, soften her heart. May she truly have a relationship with Jesus. May she come to trust you and your Word. May she come to understand that you suffered and died on the cross for her sins so she can be clean and have a relationship with you.*

It was a bright, hot, sunny late Friday afternoon at the end of August. I looked up from reading to see Pam's big black truck pull up into the parking space. As Pam got out of the truck, her face appeared downcast and serious, which was unlike her smiling self.

She took long strides until she stood in front of where I was sitting. She began, "I have to tell you something. I was arrested last night for DWI. This is the third time I've been arrested. I'll end up in Niantic."

She paused, and I asked, "Where did you go last night?" Not that it mattered.

"To a bar. I was driving home when they pulled me over." Her voice sounded more than a little irritated. "Hope you can get someone right away," she added as we began walking to the front door to start our routine. I started to question if this was the last time I would see her, at least as an employee.

"Do you have a lawyer?" I asked as I sat in the doorway of the kitchen as Pam was preparing my meal.

"No, I'll have a public defender—no money."

"When is your court date?" I felt the need to keep her talking and gather as much information as I could, but I didn't know why.

"In two weeks, September ninth, I think," came the reply.

"You know, God can see you through this if you let him."

Pam just rolled her eyes at my statement. "I'm facing a year in jail."

"Have you been in jail before?"

"Yea, for two or three months, but never a year." Obviously, the thought of being in jail to her was over-whelming. It would be for anyone.

"Have you talked to Pastor Sonny about this?"

Pam gave me a look as if to say, "You're crazy."

In reply to her look, I said, "He could pray with you. He also might have some suggestions."

But Pam was tuning me out. All she could think about was spending the next year in a dreary jail cell at Niantic Women's Prison.

It was the evening of September 8. Nobody had seen or heard from Pam since she had left my house two weeks before. As usual, I was watching the news when the phone rang. Sara got right to the point, "Nancy just called me. Pam had not come home yet, and she is worried that she won't show up in court tomorrow. She wants me to go over and pray with her! She sounds very nervous."

Pressing the button to hang up the phone, I started to pray for the intervention in the situation.

A few hours later, Sara called again. "Nancy is upset. She is beside herself, but it helped when we prayed. I talked to her about Teen Challenge, and we called Pastor Sonny and talked to him about the possibility of Pam going to Teen Challenge. He seems open to the idea and is going to call tonight to see if they have a bed available. He is planning on being in court tomorrow."

I heard of Teen Challenge, a fifteen-month residential discipleship program that works with people who have drug or alcohol issue. Their choir team had come to our church once or twice to sing praises to God and give testimonies of changed lives because of a relationship with Jesus Christ. All who testified said they have freedom from their addictions because of their relationship with Christ. Although the majority of people who enter Teen Challenge are there voluntarily, some are court-ordered.

Soon after Cleo arrived the next morning, the phone rang.

"I'm heading over to see Pam now. She showed up a few minutes ago. We have two hours to get her ready for court. I'm calling Pastor Sonny to see if he found out if

Teen Challenge has a bed available. She needs the support of her pastor to get in. I'll be in court to support her. Pray!"

I wanted to be in court to support Pam, but I had to attend a meeting with the commissioner of the Department of Social Services. As chairperson of the committee that was addressing big issues concerning the new Personal Care Assistance Waiver Program, I had obligations.

The light was blinking on the answering machine when I arrived home from my daylong meeting. It was a friendly, chipper voice, saying, "This is Pam. Praise the Lord. I'm headed for the Teen Challenge women's home now."

Obviously, a small miracle happened in the courtroom today, the details of which I would learn in a few hours. I was ecstatic, so I shouted into the air, "Thank you, Lord!"

Sure enough, about eight thirty that evening, Sara called, sounding very upbeat. "Pam is in Teen Challenge Providence, RI. Nancy and I took her there this afternoon."

"Yes, Pam called me," I replied. "What happened in court?"

"Pam was in bad shape when I got there this morning. Her clothes were filthy. It looked like she had been wearing them for a week. I helped Nancy get her undressed and in the shower. We talked to her about Teen Challenge. She has heard of it. She seemed open to the idea of going, probably because she was scared of going to jail. But she genuinely was willing to hear God's call."

"How did court go?"

"We all sat together and started praying silently. We agreed to pray for favor, open minds, and open doors. There were a number of people before Pam's name was called.

The judge seemed stern with most of the individuals who came up in front of him. Pastor Sonny was able to talk to the public defender before court began. He was the first to speak. Basically, he told the judge there was a bed available at Teen Challenge."

"How did Pam do in front of him?"

"Oh, she was very nervous. At one point he really made her nervous, saying her blood alcohol level was extraordinarily high and could have caused a severe accident. He also said he was sure that if the program didn't have such a strong counseling component, he wouldn't have suspended her sentence and sent her to Teen Challenge for eighteen months. He probably had no idea how strong a Christian component there is, but that's all right. The Lord's will was done. She knew it was the end of the line for her. If she didn't do some time, she might end up dead. Nancy and I picked up some of her clothes at the house and brought her to Providence. She was delighted and apprehensive at the same time. Pray for her. As you may have guessed, she had been involved in drugs for a number of years. She took the first step in surrendering her life to Christ today."

"Alleluia, of course I'll pray."

Oh, Sovereign Lord, maker of heaven and earth. Thank you, Lord, for being in the courtroom today. Thank you for giving the judge your wisdom. Thank you for having Pam take the first step toward having a personal relationship with you. Lord, help her get to know you through your Word, the Bible. Oh, Lord, be with her tonight.

Teen Challenge was strict concerning contact with the outside world. Usually, only families of people who are participating in the program were permitted to have any communication with them, but an exception was made in my case. After two weeks of no contact with anyone, she was able to receive letters from her mom, Pastor Sonny, and me. Pam and I wrote to each other throughout her stay at Teen Challenge.

It was thrilling for Sara and me when we went for a visit to see Pam at Teen Challenge. Her physical appearance had changed. She looked ten years younger, smiling from ear to ear, and had this glow about her. More important, her countenance and spirit had become lighter. She had surrendered to Jesus and made Him Lord of her life. In the months that were to follow, she would work on many personal and internal issues, but she had taken the first step. Jesus would help her now each step of the way.

It was Cleo's and my honor to bring Pam's mom to the graduation ceremony at New Life for Girls in Dover, Pennsylvania, which was part of the Teen Challenge experience. Pam had stayed at New Life for Girls the majority of her time in Teen Challenge. She was headed back to Providence, Rhode Island, where she would work as a staff person for the next seven years, where the Lord refined her. Eventually, the Lord called her back to live with her mom, who was getting up in years. Throughout the years, we have kept in touch and now see each other once a month for dinner and a chat.

17

Seek, Knock, Find

Ask, and it will be given to you: seek, and you will find;
knock, and it will be opened to you.

—Matthew 7:7

Pastor Gil was surely missed when he moved back to Idaho. He was originally from there and went to be with his relatives again and to contemplate life. Pastor Sonny, the new pastor, had been at Chaplin Congregational Church for approximately a year. During that year, there had been a slow but steady trickle of families leaving the church, including some of the leadership. Pastor Sonny had implemented several changes in a short amount of time.

I was stuck between a rock and a hard place. On one hand, I wanted to leave because the church had changed so much without input from the congregation. On the other hand, Pastor Sonny Raymond was mentoring Pam and my leaving Chaplin Church might raise numerous questions in her mind. This wouldn't be healthy for Pam's recovery.

When Pam left for Teen Challenge, it was as if God was releasing me from Chaplin Church, but not immediately. He wanted to make sure the relationship between Pam and Pastor Sonny had a firm foundation. One of the last things I did was to share the first letter from Pam, which was long, rambling and emotional, with Pastor Sonny.

I felt lost. Should I really leave the church I'd known for so long? Would I find a place that would accept me?

I started going to different churches. One of the first was the one Sara and John were attending at the time. They had left Chaplin Church a few months earlier. As Providence would have it, the pastor was speaking on Romans 13:1–5: "Let every soul be subject to the governing authorities. For there is no authority except from God, and the authorities that exist are appointed by God. Therefore whoever resists the authority resists the ordinance of God and those who resist will bring judgment on themselves. For rulers are not a terror to good works, but to evil. Do you want to be unafraid of the authority? Do what is good, and you will have praise from the same. For he is God's minister to you for good. But if you do evil, be afraid; for he does not bear the sword in vain; for he is God's minister, an avenger to execute wrath on him who practices evil. Therefore, you must be subject, not only because of wrath but also for conscience' sake."

As I listened, tears would sometimes well up in my eyes. I was being convicted that I could no longer attend Chaplin Church. When the service was over, men and women filed out, but I just sat there, immovable. Stephanie, who had been my assistant for a while, could tell something was going on with me but had no clue what it was. Sara spotted me and came over. She had an idea what was happening because of her own experience and involvement in the church. After the sanctuary emptied, Sara escorted me to the altar, where Evelyn, a good friend of Sara's and mine and who worked for me for a little while, joined us to pray as I poured my heart out to the Lord. Big, unwelcome, but necessary changes would be on the way in my life.

As the Bible teaches, hearers of the Word are under the authority of the one who is teaching them, usually a pastor. I was coming to realize that I could no longer be under Pastor Sonny's authority, which meant I would have to leave the church I grew up in and loved.

The search for a new church family sometimes saw me in the same congregation two or three consecutive Sundays, sometimes longer. Although I had heard a little bit about each church background, my knowledge of different denominations was limited. In one sense, it was exciting to attend a variety of churches that emphasized different aspects of Christianity, but on the other hand, it was lonely. People were friendly for the moment, but nothing beyond pleasantries. I attended a community church for six or seven months with solid biblical teaching, but there was something missing. Although there were individuals who were friendly, it was surface stuff.

The search for a church family ended approximately a year after it began. When I came home from Word of Life Family Camp in mid-August of 1998, Cookie, a new housemate who was Michelle's replacement, and Jason, the man she had her eye on, had gone to a music outreach sponsored by a local church. They were impressed with their community-mindedness and asked if I would like to attend a service. I was agreeable.

I wheeled into Abundant Life Community Church and parked myself next to some chairs for Cookie and Jason. Immediately, a woman with a broad, infectious smile came and knelt next to my chair. "My name is Joan, what's yours?" she said as she looked directly into my eyes. I'm usually leery when anyone asked that question. Due to my speech pattern, either the person will think I said "Karen" or completely misunderstand and become embarrassed. Somehow, I sensed she would be different. I was surprised when she understood my name. She explained she had a brother who had an intellectual disability. She also informed me she was a nurse at a facility right down the road from where I lived.

Joan took time to become a dear friend to me. She was a sweet, kind woman who had been walking with the Lord for many years. She had the remarkable ability to discern a situation and pinpoint what needs to happen so she could give spirit-filled advice. She genuinely cared about everyone she met, and many in the church sought her and her husband out for words of wisdom.

After attending the church a few times, I found that quite a few people took an interest in welcoming strangers who became their friend. Lynn, the pastor's wife, was one of them, although I didn't realize she was the pastor's wife for a month or two. She showed an interest in getting to know me despite her responsibilities as a mother of three sons and a daughter.

The congregation was small, so it was easier to get to know each other. It took some time to figure out what the church was all about. It wasn't a mainline denomination, which I was used to. There was no altar or platform signifying we are all equal in God's eye. A handmade wooden cross stood in the right corner of the room. It had nails on each end of the horizontal beam, signifying the suffering Jesus endured on the cross. I never saw anything quite like it, before or since. This cross was something to ponder and meditate on.

There wasn't any one moment Cookie, Jason, or I decided to make Abundant Life our church family. We just kept coming Sunday after Sunday. One thing that attracted Cookie and Jason was Jim and Pearl Barton, who brought dozens of kids from disadvantaged neighborhoods to their house after service every week. They received teaching from the Word of God, a delicious homemade meal, and much-needed mentoring. Jim and Pearl were grateful for Cookie's and Jason's assistance as they were getting up in years. The Bartons had been organizing these gatherings for over twenty years. Once in a while, a young person who had moved on in life would visit them and update them on how well they were doing, which the Bartons were grateful for.

Most organizations have a conductor who oversees and orchestrates the group. Pastor Kevin was the earthly conductor of Abundant Life, especially spiritually, but he always pointed to the ultimate Conductor, Jesus. He and several members of the congregation established the nondenominational church in October of 1988. With the

Lord's help, their desire was to create a church similar to the early church found in Acts chapter two, where everyone was filled with the Holy Spirit and people supported each other regularly. There was also an emphasis on youth because they were the future.

From the start, I found Pastor Kevin's messages to be clear and biblically sound, sprinkled with humor and stories that conveyed the point he was trying to make. He was a sensitive man who desired to assist anyone in need but went about it in a deliberate and wise way. But I got the distinct impression, although I may have been wrong, in those first few months that he felt he had to heal me or just didn't know how to interact with me. Slowly, this changed as we had discussions in small group Bible study. One evening, we had a conversation regarding the Holocaust, and I mentioned that a million people with disabilities, particularly children, were killed in gas chambers in Germany at the beginning of World War II. Pastor Kevin had a puzzled look on his face. If what I was saying was true, it was horrifying, but it appeared he had never heard of this before. I think he did some research and found it was true.

A few years after I came to Abundant Life, Pastor Kevin gave a message on the importance of water baptism. I had heard similar sermons on this topic before and had come close to asking Pastor Gil to baptize me on more than one occasion but, to my shame, always felt self-conscious. One or two people would need to carry me into the Natchug River. I didn't want to make a spectacle of myself. I finally realized it wasn't about me but was about having a deeper relationship with Jesus.

Two things penetrating my brain and heart while listening to Pastor Kevin's message: First, Jesus, the Son of God, asked John, his cousin, to baptize Him before He started His ministry. Why would I think I didn't need to be baptized because I had known Jesus for so many years when Jesus was baptized at the beginning of his ministry? Who did I think I was? This was wrong thinking. If Jesus needed to get baptized, I surely needed to do the same.

Second, he explained that baptism was not only surrendering your old, sinful life for a new one in Christ but declaring it publicly to a faith community. In my heart, I had surrendered my life to the Lord but hadn't done so publicly.

It was a warm, sunny Sunday in early August. After service, people gathered at the pond on the grounds of the Willimantic Camp Meeting Association. Previously, I had asked Jason to carry me in the water. He had carried me into his parents' house numerous times, but on that August day, he became preoccupied with Cookie, who went into labor early that morning and gave birth to twin girls, Maddie and Gabbie.

I went into a slight panic. Who would assist me into the water? Then I saw Sara and her husband, John. He assessed the situation, took off his leather belt, handed it to Sara, and proceeded to help drive my motorized chair through some sand so I could get closer to the pond. After a time of prayer, he picked me up in his strong arms, as if it was routine for him. I should have known—God had it under control. I didn't have to worry.

Cookie and Jason had left two or three years after we came to Abundant Life. As with any church or organization, individuals and families move on to other places. Both Jim and Pearl Barton and Joan and Frank moved to join their grandchildren. As of this writing, the people of Abundant Life have been my church family for over twenty years. The Lord continues to change my heart little by little to conform it to His.

18

A Pleasant Surprise
by Pastor Kevin White

Let us not become weary in doing good, for at the
proper time we will reap a harvest if we do not give up.
— Galatians 6:9 (NIV)

It was a brisk, chilly Thursday morning in New England.
It seemed that humans should not be required to go
outdoors and navigate the ice and snow on days like this.
Yet more pedestrians than I expected were gingerly making
their way up and down the sidewalk, heading for jobs and
appointments in town. Maybe it's my competitive nature,
but I like it when our church building is the first "store-
front" on Main Street to have a safe, shoveled sidewalk following a snowstorm. I think it sends a message to people in
our town that we love them and care about them.

In our church community, we try to do everything we
can as volunteers, spending money only when it is necessary for experts and craftsmen to bring their skills to repair
or improve our facility. So snow shoveling, raking, decorating, painting, carpeting, minor repairs and weekly cleaning of our church facilities is done by members who faith-

fully volunteer their time. We don't even rent a dumpster. Members bring garbage and recyclables home with them! Their generosity enables our church to direct more financial resources to community outreach and missions.

On this morning, it was taking me longer than I expected to clear a narrow path in front of our building. I thought about how nice it might be to have "the professionals" shovel after yesterday's relentless snowfall in twenty-degree weather. At the same time, I remembered the labors of dear friends at Crossroads Physical Therapy who recently helped me overcome a shoulder injury. I was also grateful for the prayers of people in our church community during that ordeal, including one person who regularly prays for me. I call her CJ (short for Carolyn Jean). What a joy to be able to shovel at all.

The snow was packed down and *heavy*. Having arrived with only a single snow shovel, a thought occurred to me after fifteen minutes of very slow progress on the sidewalk. Why not go inside and grab the ice chopper that was sitting in the church storage closet? Maybe even warm up for a few minutes. That could certainly make my task easier. But the front door lock was frozen shut. So much for that idea.

Eventually, finally, the path was cleared for the length of our building. Although only one pedestrian could walk in only one direction at a time, and it probably was not yet up to the Americans with Disabilities Act standards, my lower back was telling me it was time to head home and find a heating pad. Soon! As A.A. Milne's Winnie-the-Pooh character was once quoted as saying, "Sometimes I sits and thinks, and sometimes I just sits…"

At home, I rewarded myself with breakfast, then a trip to my favorite living room chair and heating pad. As the skies cleared, my wonderful wife, Lynn, and terrific son, Joseph, volunteered to travel to the church building to start clearing the back steps and to widen and finish my efforts on the front sidewalk. Off they went.

An hour or two later, they returned and told me about a pleasant surprise they had on their journey. When they arrived at the church, the lights were on, and the front door was unlocked! CJ and her cleaning crew were inside, volunteering their precious time to make sure the building was cleaned for a special event coming up on Saturday.

How did they get in? I know the apostles were able to break out of a jail once. Now, I discovered that CJ is able to break into a building that was frozen and locked to me. I shouldn't have been surprised. I've seen her determination and persistence on many occasions, but what a pleasant surprise it was.

But wait. I had only cleared a narrow path on the sidewalk. How did she navigate that? I'm not sure mathematically how that happened. So I'll just say again, persistence and determination! What else? And what is a person with a physical disability doing volunteering to clean the church facility once every month in the first place? Yes, one more time—determination, persistence. And how about perseverance?

I've witnessed many people, even those who are followers of Jesus, come up with reasons why they can't do this or can't do that. I've even traveled down that road more than once. You know, pretending I have a good reason for why

I wasn't doing the very things that I knew I could do—and should do. We might even invent clever words and phrases to justify our actions, like "opt out." Or "I don't feel led."

But thankfully, I have never witnessed that behavior in CJ. Not after nearly two decades of knowing her. And that inspires me. It encourages me. See, if I neglect getting started, or decide to quit before I arrive, I really have nobody to blame but me. God lets us make choices, but he also has us own them. My choices are my responsibility.

CJ would rightfully tell you that this is God's grace at work in her life and that all the credit should go to Jesus. I agree. But this snowy story is just one of many occasions where I have seen CJ refuse to find an excuse. Instead, she finds a way.

Carolyn is a faithful prayer partner every week when we gather on Wednesdays to pray for people in our church and community. Most of all, she is a dear and trusted friend, not only to my wife, myself, and our family, but to many others as well. CJ has an eye for people who need a little bit of extra encouragement. She "conspires" to be a blessing to them. She finds ways to schedule her helpers to bring her to church and fellowship where they can hear the gospel and testimonies from other believers.

As a result, I have seen firsthand how people's lives have changed because of the investment Carolyn chose to make in them. Her actions have shown that she takes seriously these words of Scripture: "Let us not become weary in doing good, for at the proper time we will reap a harvest if we do not give up" (Galatians 6:9 NIV).

CJ is also a positive "provocateur." What is that? I love the King James version of Hebrews, especially as I see it at work in her life. Because of the grace of God at work in us, may you and I, as well as Carolyn, live out these words of Scripture: "Let us hold fast the profession of our faith without wavering; (for He is faithful that promised;) and let us consider one another to *provoke* unto love and to good works: not forsaking the assembling of ourselves together, as the manner of some is; but exhorting one another: and so much the more, as ye see the day approaching" (Hebrews 10:23–25).

19

Dark Days

Jesus said to him, "I am the way,
and the truth, and the life."

—John 14:6a

Dark clouds had rolled in the day before the calendar turned to 2006. The clouds started slowly to accumulate during that autumn, but now the storm was here. I didn't realize what a whirlwind it would be.

On the morning of New Year's Eve, Glen called to inform me that Mom had passed on to the arms of Jesus. I had deluded myself to thinking I was ready when Mom passed away because Mom wasn't Mom anymore. The delusion dissolved that day. I couldn't understand why I was so sad. The essence or soul of Mom seemed to have disappeared years ago, but the death of that body was so final.

There was the usual flurry of activity as we prepared for the memorial service. Then we went back to our lives, or so it seemed. As the year progressed, I got a vague uneasiness when I was working. I had been employed by the

Disabilities Network for seventeen years and had steered it through many tough times as well as some victories. For many years, we were like family, who sometimes squabbled and had our disagreements, but for the most part, we all got along.

Like most organizations, the Disabilities Network changed over time. Some staff and board members came and went while others remained a fixture of DNEC for years. In the early 2000s, we moved our rickety office from Franklin to the city of Norwich, which increased our professionalism, including having separate offices for all the staff.

While this move increased our profile and had other advantages, the atmosphere of the office changed slowly over time. By the late spring and early summer, I knew something was amiss. I had hired an employee who didn't work out. Although it wasn't the first time I had fired someone, it was the first time someone filed a discrimination complaint with the State of Connecticut against DNEC. Two staff members offered to organize a second annual tag sale, which I agreed to but regretted after learning there would be a booth for tarot card reading, which I wouldn't have approved of if I had a say, but somehow I didn't. Deep down inside I recognized I was losing control of the organization.

When September came, Cleo, who had been my personal assistant at work since I had become executive director, and I were asked to attend a special board meeting. At this meeting, I was asked to resign or I would be fired. Cleo was also let go. I was crushed. My world had just fallen apart by accusations and lies. The past didn't matter. I suspected two staff members were behind this cue for political reasons. They wanted a change to a person with a mental health disability at the helm of DNEC and had convinced the board of directors that I did some misdeeds. My suspicions became reality the Monday after my departure when one of the suspected persons became interim director and someone with a mental health disability became the permanent director. Curiously enough, one of the misdeeds that I was accused of committing was rectified when the item in question mysteriously appeared.

I spent the next month or two mulling over and over and over about what had just happened, the injustices that had occurred. Where did I go wrong? Was I too open with the staff? Too careless? And what was the "truth" anyway?

I didn't completely recognize it at the time, but I had lost my identity. For over seventeen years, I had been an executive director and disability rights advocate, had chaired numerous councils, and was recognized on the federal level for an innovative initiative for youth who were transitioning from high school to adult life. None of that mattered. I had failed. What do I do for the rest of my life?

One Sunday morning, as usual, I woke up before my assistant came to get me up. Part of me wanted to pull up the sheets or crawl in a hole, which is very unlike my personality. In that moment, not completely aware of it, I was at a crossroad. I could press on, "run with endurance the race that is set before us," as Paul encourages every Christian to do in Hebrews 12:2, or crawl into a hole of doubt and depression. I didn't consciously make a decision, but believed that the Holy Spirit had guided me through that difficult season.

Exploring employment online, which was necessary to receive unemployment compensation, was a challenge. There was only a part-time position for an Americans with Disabilities Act coordinator that looked like a possibility, but after the interview, I had my doubts. My doubts were correct.

More important, I started to study the Bible more. The question "What is truth?" kept repeating in my mind. One Sunday I asked Penny, who had, for a period, with her husband, Tim, opened up their home to a weekly Bible study, for some verses on "truth". I looked up several verses but pondered a familiar one: "Jesus said to him, 'I am the way, and the truth, and the life'" (John 14:6a). It struck me. This verse was saying Jesus is the truth. The truth is a person, the Son of God. Usually, we think of facts as the truth, but those facts can be twisted. Jesus embodies the ultimate truth.

Obviously, my life would change. One of my first choices in that change was to peruse the Bible to know Jesus more deeply and to serve him. I started to attend prayer and Bible study regularly on Wednesday evenings. Sometimes the emphasis was on prayer, and other times we did a video series on a biblical topic. Shortly after I started attending regularly, we studied the topic "Who I Am in Christ," thanks to Pastor Kevin. Two or three weeks into the series, it dawned on me that the topic was picked for my benefit. I had to refocus my identity. As with everyone who believes Jesus is the Son of God, I am a child of God, I'm precious to Him and have value.

I was watching the news one evening, and there was a heartbreaking segment on a man who shot eleven school-age children, killing five of them. It took place in Nickel Miles, Pennsylvania, which is Amish country. A grandparent gave the man much grace by forgiving the man who murdered their grandchild the afternoon of the shooting. Community members reached out to the murderer's family with compassion. What an example to the world.

I had more business to take care of. That night, lying in bed, praying, the Sermon on the Mount came to mind. This is where Jesus instructs His disciples to love their enemies and pray for them. Jesus was instructing me to pray for the two staff members, but there was more to it. Pondering and praying about this for a while, I realized a letter of forgiveness to the DNEC board was my next assignment from the Lord. For this task, I recruited three trusted persons to keep me on the straight and narrow as far as the wording of the letter. No bitterness or accusations should be contained in the letter, only forgiveness and closure. I continued to pray, and it occurred to me that forgiveness is an ongoing process instead of a onetime event.

Little by little, my emotional scars began to heal. One of my friends from church, a special education teacher named Candy, started visiting me for "elocution lessons." She wanted, for some reason, to understand my speech better. As we talked, we became good friends who shared personal thoughts and feeling. Those conversations helped me refocus on others. She had invested time in a man after her husband had gone to be with the Lord, but the relationship fell apart. We talked through that and many other things.

We also explored working on a project together. She had arranged a daylong trip to New York to take a tour of a home that assists women with addiction issues to get them back on their feet physically, mentally, and spiritually. But out of nowhere, so it seemed, she went in a different direction.

Slowly the clouds were dispersing. The sun was peeking out. What would be my new adventure?

20

A Walk of Grace Includes Carolyn
by Candy Wilks

I first met Carolyn in 2003 when I moved to the sleepy little Quiet Corner of northeast Connecticut. Carolyn and I were attending the same church. There was something different about Carolyn that made me want to get to know her at a friend level, not just as fellow church attendees. She had the most unusual circle of friends that admired and cared for her. There was a level of respect toward Carolyn that told me, "This is a quality gal." So with that in mind, I set out to discover all the valuable virtues (and not trinkety junk) that was in Carolyn's treasure chest.

We began by meeting once a week for "elocution lessons." I had heard that term from the movie *Singing in the Rain.* One character needed this type of lesson to tame her shrewd, ear-numbing singing and make her voice pleasant in song. In this case, it was I who needed the lessons to tune my sensory muscles for clearer understanding. Carolyn patiently repeated phrases, spelled words, and waited for a light to come on in my command central. Gradually, our communication was easier and our friendship grew through understanding each other's inflections, words and moods.

Carolyn has brought a deeper level of compassion and understanding to my world. Although I've worked in the world of disabilities for many years, my perception became sharper and keener. Carolyn and I went to dinner one night with several other single adults around our age. We enjoyed ourselves, engaging in chatter with the others and eating delicious food. At the end of our meal, we expected the server to deliver our checks to us. Everyone else around us received their checks and went to pay at the cash register. When it was evident that our checks had not been deposited to us, I said to Carolyn, "We didn't get our checks."

Carolyn said, "I know. I think someone paid for us." The benefactor did not divulge who they were, so we gathered our belongings and started out the door. Before we could get to Carolyn's van (the van is retrofitted for a lift and Carolyn's motorized chair), a gentleman sprinted up to us. He gave me a huge hug and commented, "I think it's just wonderful the way *these* people can get out nowadays."

I said to him, "Carolyn and I are *friends*. This is her van, I'm just driving it tonight." I tried a few more times to convince him Carolyn was not a charity case and I was not her caregiver. He obviously was not listening and had little concept of what he was talking about. The man turned around and walked back into the restaurant very satisfied with himself.

I said to Carolyn, "I think he thinks we're from a facility."

Carolyn displayed much more grace than did I. She said, "He probably paid for our food," and then she was going to let it go. I was shocked by such ignorant yet well-meaning behavior. It made me mad, yet Carolyn took it in stride.

"Doesn't this kind of behavior bother you?" I asked Carolyn on the ride home, my feathers still ruffled.

"No," she said. "I've had things like this happen all my life. I've never been any other way."

I began to get a glimpse into my friend's world. She has had people treat her this way her whole life.

On another occasion, we were in a well-known restaurant. We had been seated and given menus, which we were perusing, and were waiting for the server to take our orders. The very young man arrived at our table, disheveled and already befuddled. He introduced himself and asked me what I would like to drink. He took my order and then asked me, "What does she want to drink?" nodding at Carolyn.

I looked back at him, confused, and said, "I don't know. You have to ask her."

The young server very loudly said, "WHAT WOULD YOU LIKE TO DRINK?"

Again, I was met with confusion. Why would you yell at someone who is capable of hearing you? It seemed like a valid question to me.

Carolyn politely said, "Root beer." Since I knew it is Carolyn's favorite soda, I repeated it for the server.

After he left to get our drinks, I asked my friend, "That didn't bother you?"

"No, I deal with it all the time."

I wanted to "educate" the lad upon return, but Carolyn helped me be more gracious. We chuckled about my ignorance with the boy. Carolyn is like that.

Our server retuned with our drinks. He was ready with his pad and pen to take our orders. I placed my order, and then he did it again. Mind you, Carolyn had a menu in front of her and was looking at it intently.

"What does she want to eat?" the youngster asked. I gave him an exasperated sigh.

"She has a menu. You'll have to ask her," was all I could manage to say without being rude.

He turned to Carolyn, and again, with his outdoor voice, said, "WHAT DO YOU WANT TO EAT?"

Carolyn told him what she wanted and I repeated it for him. He took our menus and was off to place the order.

This was lesson night for me. My friend's world has been one with challenges, hurdles, and kerfuffles. Yet my friend learned early on to be gracious and, when misunderstood, be the understanding one. Carolyn showed me how to handle these situations correctly.

Carolyn and I have had our differences of opinion. We began working on a project together that was long term and large scale. We had a vision and worked well together. I have to take the responsibility for the project not materializing. Through some choices I made, our friendship suffered, and I became very closed off. Carolyn adjusted to the choices, and our friendship, although not the same, endured.

We no longer worked on the project together and our lives took different directions. Again, Carolyn was gracious, extending kindness and caring. I lived with the consequences of my choice and made the best of it. Carolyn tried to penetrate the force field, but I had made my bed and didn't expect anyone to bail me out. It was a very sad and dark time for me. Carolyn waited on the outside all the while. Sometimes we punish ourselves worse than anyone else ever could. I'm certain plenty of prayers went from Carolyn's house on my behalf.

It took a few years, but when I started to see clearly, my friend's patience paid off. I missed our times together. And we started Friday Girls' Praise and Prayer. Five to six ladies gather on Friday nights for a potluck-type meal and prayer. Our little group has grown and shrunk, but God has been faithful to answer prayer. Sometimes on occasion, we have had men attend our little group also. One young man came to our group several months. We were his aunties, mommies, and grammies. We welcomed, doted on, and fed him. It was a pleasure to be able to provide grace to him when he needed it. This group has been valuable to all who attend. We celebrate birthdays and holidays. Nobody is forgotten. Grace…

I really love our Christmas celebrations. This year we celebrated on Three Kings Day. We don't purchase gifts for each other. The gifts are homemade or something we already have. Our newest member received meaningful gifts that spoke to her personally. It was a beautiful occasion. It was unhurried, inexpensive, and relaxing. Carolyn orchestrates with her hospitality gift she says she doesn't have. But it's so obvious to everyone else that she shines like a hospitality star. My hope is this continues for many years and touches many more sisters and the occasional brother.

Carolyn's circle of friends includes all kinds of people, including some rough-around-the-edges teens that she's allowed me to bring to her house. Carolyn teaches these kids some valuable vocational and life skills. There was a particular young man who took a liking to Carolyn. He would say to me when it was time to leave her house, "I don't want to leave Carolyn. She needs me!" He worked hard at whatever Carolyn had for him to do. He grew to think of Carolyn as a family member. He said about Carolyn, "There's no difference between Carolyn and other people. Inside, Carolyn wants what everybody else wants." There are many other teens who see something about Carolyn and respond. It's the grace she treats everyone with. It's a subtle compassion in the way she listens, speaks, and understands. Then she prays for the person and remembers to follow up with them when she can. The teens I bring to Carolyn's house, more often than not, leave with not only job readiness and vocational skills, but life skills as well. They gain a respect for people by listening to Carolyn, completing a task correctly—even if it means doing it again.

21

Round Two

And we all, with unveiled face, beholding[b] the
glory of the Lord, are being changed into His
likeness from one degree of glory to another;
for this comes from the Lord who is the Spirit.

—2 Corinthians 3:18

Cleo hit the button on the answering machine. "Hi, I'm
Sheila. I used to work for you a few years ago. I saw
your ad in the paper for a roommate. I'm interested." For
some reason, I instantly recognized her voice.

She had worked every other weekend for approximately a year. I couldn't remember if she had quit or just
not showed up one weekend. I remember her energetic,
bubbly personality. She lived in Willimantic with someone
named Larry, who had a brain injury.

My current housemate, Ketsya, who had lived with me
for four years and had just graduated from the University of
Connecticut School of Pharmacy, was moving to Chicago
to start her career. As usual, I had placed an ad in *The*

Chronicle but had received only one other response. After interviewing the woman, I was praying another person would answer the ad. We had arranged to have the interview on the lawn at a friend's house because she had no transportation. She seemed to be going through a difficult time at the moment, but I had an uneasy sense some of her troubles were brought upon by herself. I suspected she was involved in drugs. She was very thin, and her eyes didn't always focus.

It was a warm early August morning when Sheila came for the interview. Cleo opened the door to a tallish woman with curly light-brown hair, wearing a T-shirt and blue denim shorts. The interview quickly turned into a catch-up conversation about old friends, with questions sprinkled here and there relating to the situation at hand.

I had vaguely remembered Sheila had a daughter named Jocelyn, who was now 12.

"Can she stay over on the weekends?" Sheila asked. "She is a good girl, quiet."

I thought it was an odd question and wanted to ask why she didn't live with her permanently, but didn't want to pry into personal matters.

Sheila did explain that she had been living with an elderly woman who had passed away two weeks ago. The family wanted to put the house on the market by the end of the month. She appeared anxious about finding a place to live. She tapped her pen on the table giving a general sense of uneasiness.

Monet, my cat, walked by, which gave a perfect opportunity for her to change the subject. "Pretty kitty," Sheila said in a high-pitched voice as she reached out to pet the gray fur ball.

"She is the queen," I explained.

"Oh, I have a black-and-white cat named Toby. He is old, twelve, so he won't bother anyone. I've had him since he was a kitten. He is my Toby. If I live here, can he come too?"

"Yes," I replied, "if you move in, you can bring your cat." I try as much as possible to be accommodating, but how the Queen would react to another cat invading her territory was another question. Four years ago, I adopted Silly Head, who was Amanda's, another housemate of mine. Three felines might be pushing it, but I seem to be a sucker for those furry creatures.

We went over her duties, which included putting me to bed six nights a week, getting me up, dressing me, and giving me breakfast and lunch on Saturdays and taking me somewhere fun once a month. This seems to fit nicely into her Tri-County ARC work schedule.

Tri-Country ARC operates several group homes and day programs for individuals who have intellectual disabilities. Sheila worked in a group home in Tolland two or three days a week and was one-on-one with a woman who had her own apartment in Willimantic.

After Sheila moved in, we quickly settled into a routine. She was constantly on the go, but she made sure to be home promptly by 10:30 p.m. to assist me to bed.

Sheila grew up in the Christian faith. Her father went to Bible college in upstate New York when she was a child.

So as part of our snack before bed, she would read out load the corresponding Proverb for that day's date.

My first clue something was amiss came one Sunday while someone was feeding me lunch. Sheila briskly walked in the door with a friend, said a few pleasantries, and went quickly upstairs. I've seen the glass-eyed look before, an indication the person is using illegal substances. For the moment, I dismissed it, but it was filed in my memory.

One evening in early October, Sheila came downstairs crying. Memories were flooding her soul. I sat there for what seemed like an hour holding her while she poured out her heart. Sheila told of growing up in the projects in Bridgeport, Connecticut, where she heard gunshots frequently. She told details of her brother's suicide on July 4th a number of years ago. She also described some of the many hospitalizations she experienced. It was one of those rehabilitation experiences that brought her to Willimantic.

The next day, I called Sara. She might have some ideas on how to help Sheila. By this time, she had become friends with Sara's family, particularly her daughter, Amy. Amy's husband, Aaron, had similar issues to Sheila, so he could relate to her on a different level.

After a conversation with Amy, Sara came to the condo, and we jointly invited Sheila to attend a Tres Dias weekend. By God's grace, it would put her on the correct path in life. She had a great time and made friends with several people, including a girl in her twenties. She also became close to Margaret Payne, one of the loyal, long-time members of our chapter. They had a common experience of working with people with cognitive disabilities. Sheila and Margret created a bond that weekend that would have great benefits.

As the November winds blew, one day Sheila called to say she voluntarily went into a psychiatric unit and would be there for five days. She would need someone to pick her up. I was disappointed but not surprised. She had been hospitalized so many times but usually short term and in a secular setting. Change is made over time. From observing Sheila for the past few months, I came to the conclusion that she had a great deal of head knowledge about the Bible but something was blocking it from getting to her heart.

One night in early March, the phone rang. It was Sheila telling me she was in Hartford and couldn't come home because she was "wasted." Fortunately, Cookie and Jason had just rented a place a mile or so from my condo, so I called Cookie to put me to bed. Lying in bed, I prayed for Sheila's protection as she was in a crack house and pondered what to do next.

Waking up early the next morning, I started praying. Sheila would be coming home and I needed some idea of what to say to her. I heard her open the front door and close it, then immediately, she came and sat on my bed. Tears were streaming down her face. "That's it, I'm done. I surrender to God." Those were the words I wanted to hear, but more sufficiently, those were the words Jesus longed to hear. Many have the idea that surrendering is a onetime event, but those who know Jesus well know that it can be a daily, sometimes hourly, occurrence.

Was she serious? We talked a bit. Sheila did most of the talking. She had known about Teen Challenge for several years. She knew who Pam was and they had a few conversations over a period of some years. Pam encouraged her to enter the program, but Sheila always had declined. So when I said, "Call Pam," I waited with bated breath.

She dialed the number I had memorized using the phone next to the bed. This meant the conversation would be on speakerphone. Pam answered the phone at that early hour. Sheila repeated her desire to surrender herself to Jesus, to give her life to him. Pam gave her some suggestions and gave her the number of Teen Challenge in Providence. She called them and got the ball rolling while still sitting on my bed, so I heard the information.

Sheila came downstairs in the early afternoon and immediately started slamming kitchen cabinet doors. Under her breath but loud enough for me to hear, she said, "Eighteen months, too long, not going." Although I was a novice when it came to spiritual warfare, I recognized that this was an example of it. I prayed for protection, wisdom, and discernment.

The next two weeks proved to be challenging. Sheila decided not to enter a facility to detox. Friends like Amy, Candy, and others came to support her. With medical appointments, paperwork, preparing to be away for a long time, and keeping her from the streets, she needed the support. By the grace of God, everything was completed just in time.

The day before she would enter Teen Challenge was a Sunday. As usual, she attended church with Amy and her family. After my assistant gave me lunch and left, I started to work on my computer, but I couldn't. This thought was compelling me: "Call Sheila." There wasn't any reason to do so. It was like something inside me that wasn't me, the Holy Spirit, was directing my thoughts. I hit the button to speed-dial her cell number. Her voice sounded light pitched, like she was about to cry or had been crying. We talked for a minute or two. Upon hanging up the phone, my thumb pressed the number to call Cookie. I told her to call Amy. Amy didn't understand my speech well and time was of the essence. Amy was just a few streets away from where Sheila was. All the way to get her, Amy kept talking. From the moment I called her until she entered the doors of Teen Challenge, there was an imminent possibility Sheila would use again. Sheila was about to use the moment I called her.

As we entered the Teen Challenge house, I noticed numerous structural changes that had been made since my visit with Pam ten years ago. We would learn there were other changes. In the two weeks prior, we had to secure the first month's boarding fee, as well as a list of monthly financial supporters, including Sheila's newly made friend, Margret Payne.

Amy and I signed papers and committed that visitors that came to see her had to come with one of us. This included any family member who wanted to see her. She could have visitors every two weeks. This meant an hour-long trip one way, an hour or so visiting time, then back home. One of the purposes of these visits with family members was to resolve issues and reconcile relationships. Sheila and her daughter had issues to work out. Some of those times, visiting tended to be on the awkward side.

Sheila stayed exactly two years, two months, and two days in Teen Challenge, as she would fondly emphasize. She often described it as "Christian boot camp." There was strict discipline, getting up before dawn, going to bed late, chapel time, studying the Bible, as well as working in the community. She enjoyed evangelizing on the streets but not on those bitter cold days when the wind whipped around. Her compassionate heart for the homeless and hurting kept her going.

After her graduation, she stayed as a mentor for six months to speak into the lives of the women who entered Teen Challenge after her. She came back to the Willimantic area, obtained her EMT license, and in 2016 opened her own business, called CPR Alive. She teaches first aid, CPR instruction, and teaches some survival courses to local businesses and state agencies, and she even has contracts from out of state. By God's grace, she has achieved her goals and serves Jesus.

22

The Blue House

And He (Jesus) said, "It is written, 'My
house shall be a house of prayer.'"
—Luke 20:47

After Sheila went into Teen Challenge, Cookie agreed
to put me to bed until I found another housemate.
She, Jason, and their three young children had moved into
a house they were renting a few months earlier. It happened
to be a mile from the condo.

One night shortly after Sheila left, Cookie came over
with a proposal. She and Jason were considering becoming
missionaries, but they had just decided not to go into the
mission field at this time. Would I consider buying a house
with them? She gave me some time to pray about it before
giving her an answer.

A few years earlier, Sara and her husband, John, had
talked about building an addition to their house. I was
tired of changing housemates ever year or two. We would
develop a relationship with each other, become attached

to each other, then it would be time for her to move on to another chapter of her life. Then there are the ones who don't work out, who don't come home to put me to bed, or who stay up half the night in the living room, running up my phone bill. But the Lord decided to take John home after a fight with lung cancer.

Lying there that night, I started praying, but my prayers were interrupted by exciting thoughts and wondering what the future holds. Over time, my prayer became, "Open the doors you want opened and close the doors you want closed. Your will be done." I never received a direct "go ahead" or "no" from Jesus, but doors began to open.

Jason, Cookie, and I were preapproved for a mortgage. To keep it all in the family, Sara was our realtor, and Aaron, Jason's brother-in-law, agreed to build the addition or renovate a garage, whatever was necessary. Cookie, Jason, and I took trips around Mansfield, the town the condo was in, so we knew it fairly well.

After considering two or three other houses, we settled on a blue house on the main road going from Willimantic to the University of Connecticut campus. This wasn't my ideal location, but by God's grace, the house was set off the road with beautiful landscaping and a large backyard surrounded by woods. Before we bought the house, I tested out the thirty-five-degree slope on the side of the house, which went down into the backyard. It was scary trying it for the first time, but my chair made it back up the incline just fine. This became my refuge and reading spot in summers.

It was a steamy day in mid-July when I moved into that blue two-story house. I had recruited Amanda, an energetic housemate who used to live with me, to assist in keeping things organized and efficient. A storage space had been rented to keep most of my furniture while Aaron built an in-law efficiency apartment using the attached garage as the frame. In the meantime, my living space was the living room and dining room. Fortunately, there was a finished basement, which was made into a family room with a huge TV.

The first few weeks went pretty well. We enjoyed each other's company when we had a chance to talk. Jason was away working in New York City much of the time. This left Cookie taking care of the three children most of the time during the week.

For ten years, Cleo and I, with some friends, went camping every year in early August. That year was no exception. When I came home, I was greeted with the news that Monet, my gray long-haired cat, had disappeared. Jason had searched the neighborhood to no avail. Needless to say, I was saddened but realized having two big dogs in the house, named Samson and Goliath, didn't help Monet's peace of mind.

A few weeks later, Toby, Sheila's older feline friend, also disappeared. We began to wonder if someone in the neighborhood was keeping cats in a barn or garage. One hot day in September, I was chasing the shade and reading on the far corner of the property line in the backyard when I heard a meow. I looked down, and there was Monet, as if saying, "I love you. I miss you, but I can't be with you." She stayed for a minute then was gone, never to be seen again. In a sense, this was a foreshadowing of what was to come.

My spiritual antennas went up a few weeks after living with Cookie and Jason. One Sunday morning Cookie and Jason were having a conversation concerning where to go to church. I found out they had just left one church and were trying another. This wasn't the first time they had changed churches in the past few years. It didn't affect me much, as my assistants, Dianna or Heather, took me to Abundant Life. Wise individuals know that the spiritual aspects of a person affect the whole person.

Then one day in early September, while eating my lunch, Cleo and I heard the door slam, reverberating throughout the house. We looked at each other, as if to say, "What was that all about?" Fortunately, the three kids were in school. After Cleo left, Jason came downstairs and put one foot on the kitchen chair to tie his shoe. Our eyes met, and I saw someone whose soul had just been crushed. No words were exchanged, but something profound had taken place in their bedroom. Jason went to his mom's sometime during that day but never slept in the house again.

Over the next few months, some negative qualities were revealed concerning both Cookie and Jason. Jason, who was a soft-spoken man, was a people pleaser. Cookie was very creative and was a fabulous cook. She inherited her mom's ability to sew anything she put her mind to. Jason desired to please his wife, but over a period of years, she seemed to be never satisfied.

Shortly after his father passed away from lung cancer, Jason started drinking. Like his father, he was a functional alcoholic. For several years, only his wife knew his secret.

Of course, Cookie was devastated. She had to keep herself together for the sake of her children, Nic, Gabby, and Maddie, but after they were tucked in bed, she would let her guard down. After she put me in bed, she would lie on top of the covers and cry, talk, and pray.

At first, Jason would come to see the children, talk to Cookie, and sometimes have a conversation with me. He would reassure me he would come home soon, but as the weeks went by, doubts started to creep into my brain.

I started to question if I messed up on the decision I made to buy the house with Cookie and Jason. I asked God, "Why? Where did I go wrong?" Jesus never gave me a direct answer, but he did plant a verse in my heart. Jesus said, "My house shall be called a house of prayer" (Matthew 21:13). Although he was referring to a particular temple, he wanted me to apply it personally.

As their marriage disintegrated, I discovered another reason why I was living in the house. It was to be a stabilizing influence. There needed to be a second pair of eyes and ears to ensure there was food in the house and the bills were paid. Or was I rationalizing the decision?

There is a well-known and popular verse in Christian circles that is often quoted: "And we know that all things work together for good to those who love God, to those who are the called according to His purpose" (Romans 8:28). Although this is a beloved verse of many, including myself, it is difficult to see His purposes in a dark situation. Sometimes only when the situation is over, perhaps years later or in eternity, will we know His purpose.

Each of the children coped with the situation differently. Nic would spend hours in the basement on WIE or other video games. He was enthusiastic about being on the Little League football team and excited to wear his cleats, knee pads, and all that goes into wearing a football uniform. Like any child, he didn't like his mother's constant reminders to bring his football paraphernalia to school.

I found it curious that shortly after Jason had left, Gabby started to sweep the kitchen quite often, which was an odd activity for a six-year-old. When Jason came one day, I inquired about it. He explained that whenever they went anywhere as a family, they needed to make sure the house was clean first. "That is where it might be coming from. She might be thinking if she sweeps, I will come back home." Much of the time she spent out in the backyard, jumping on the trampoline with her siblings or in the room, which she shared with her sister.

Maddie would spend hours in front of the TV. She sometimes looked like she was in another world. It was her way of coping with the situation.

I was concerned for each one of them for various reasons. Much prayer was needed.

A fine line had to be navigated between not only Cookie and Jason but the entire Sabo family. I would hear things that I knew weren't true, things that were exaggerated, and things that were so confusing or contradictory it would make my head spin or my heart drop.

Jason came for a visit on November 6. It was Nic's birthday. After Jason visited with the kids upstairs, probably tucking them into bed, I thought nothing of it, when I saw Cookie and Jason walk outside in the cold late-fall air. Her face was bright red when she came into the kitchen and blurted out, "I just hit my husband with a two by four." I just looked at her, not knowing what to say. She retreated to the master bedroom. We learned later that Nic saw the incident, which, in my opinion, marred him for life.

November wasn't all doom and gloom. In the middle of the month, Aaron finished the in-law apartment, which I was delighted with. After five months of living in two rooms, using a commode, and sharing kitchen, I had my space. My living room was part of the main house with a door separating the in-law apartment. This room was darker than what I would have liked because of the wood paneling, but it helped me keep tabs on what was going on in the main part of house.

One of the delights of Christmas was Cookie and me taking the kids to a drive-in Christmas light festival that had various scenes, such as Santa Claus and his reindeer, a huge Christmas tree with gifts all around it, elves busy making toys, and a gingerbread house. We heard squeals of delight from the twins, but Nic wasn't so impressed. Unfortunately, a Christmas tree wasn't put up and decorated in the living room because Cookie and the kids went to Pennsylvania to be with her family for the holidays.

As the new year began, it brought a much-needed reprieve and a downhill slide. A court sheriff knocked at the front door one early afternoon and handed Cookie an envelope, which brought tears to her eyes, anger to her soul, and increased the uncertainty in the house. The envelope contained divorce papers Jason had filed.

Shortly before or after the knock on the door, Cookie reverted back to her given name, which was Becky. Jason had given her the nickname Cookie when he first met her cooking for a mission for the homeless in Philadelphia. Although most of us in Connecticut knew her real name was Becky, it was difficult to have it roll off the tongue.

Always thoughtful, Cleo invited me to spend a few days in Florida while she and her husband, Pete, visited his sister. They had asked me once or twice before, and it was always an enjoyable stay, although sleeping on the coach isn't my favorite thing in the word. They drove down, and I would fly. Usually, they met me at the gate, but this time it turned out to be an adventure. The airport staff informed Cleo and Pete they couldn't go to the gate to meet me. I was told to stay in a particular spot. I had a note with Cleo's cell number that the stewardess didn't pay any attention to. After five or ten minutes, I looked around. Seeing no airport personnel, I put my motorized wheelchair on a faster speed, then went up the ramp to the terminal. They were there at the top of the ramp waiting patiently.

Most of my time in the Sunshine State was spent taking walks around the neighborhood, enjoying the bright, warm sun and reading. I brought a book someone had recommended I read. It was written by a psychologist and, as I read it, fit the situation to a tee. It gave me insight and a bit of understanding into what was going on in the house.

Every year, Pastor Kevin does a sermon series on a book of the Bible. That year, he chose Jonah. Most people automatically think of Jonah in the belly of the whale, but there is more to the story. Jonah was a prophet who was running away from God. God had told him to go to Nineveh to preach repentance, but he went in the opposite direction. Jason was doing the same thing. He was running away from God, his family, and involvement in ministry. There were times when his family didn't know where he was for months at a time. Right before buying the house, Jason and Becky had contemplated becoming missionaries with Open Doors.

There were so many parallels between the story of Jonah and Jason it made my heart break. During each service, I would end up crying for the broken lives all around me. While Jason was running away from God, Becky seemed to be headed in the same direction at a slower pace.

Sometime that spring, Becky asked me if we could sell the house and move back to the condo, which UConn students were renting. She and the kids would live in two bedrooms upstairs. But all one had to do was to drive down the road and see five or six "for sale" signs to know this wasn't the time to sell a house. The nation was in what would be called "the great recession of 2008–2009." Consulting with a few people, I decided to rent out rooms after Becky and the kids moved to Pennsylvania in July.

Becky waited until the end of the school year to make the big move. Although this was still a difficult time, there were some bright spots. The most memorable was a trip to the Butterfly Conservatory and Gardens in Deerfield, Massachusetts. Gabby and Maddie were enthralled as the butterflies flew around us as we walked pathways that had numerous varieties of tropical plants. Nic, on the other hand, was bored and made that known. It was worth his little comments to see the look of delight on the girls' faces.

Two weeks before Becky and the kids were to move, the tension seemed to be rising. She had started packing, and her mom, a sweet, friendly, creative woman, was coming to help. Lying in bed one night, I felt my body so tensed. I realized I couldn't stay in the house. Watching Becky and her mom pack all the belongings would be too hard emotionally and, in some ways, physically.

The next morning, I told Cleo to pack some of my things, and we headed to Sara's house. I was impolite by not calling her first, but at that point, manners were down on my list of priorities. Jason was staying there and I wanted to talk to him. For one thing, I wanted to know if he was willing to carry me in and out of the house. Aaron quickly came up with a solution by building a ramp out of plywood. It wouldn't comply to any building code, but it worked, and Aaron's boys loved it, using it as a skateboard ramp long after I left.

For two weeks I slept in Sara's bed while she slept on the couch, which was unfair, but she insisted. I also inconvenienced all of my assistants because Sara's house was a longer distance to drive. They seemed to understand the situation and gave me grace.

We all should give to others the precious grace that God has given us, an undeserved favor. Sometimes we can give the grace of God incognito by praying for them.

23

Conversing with Carolyn
by Steve Timmons

I (Steve) first "met" Carolyn in 2006 when I started going to the same church as her. I put *met* in quotation marks because I did not really formally introduce myself to her, nor did I really interact with her much during those first few years, but I was attending the same church as her, so I knew she existed.

I heard amazing stories about her, and I saw lots of women at our church share many times how much they were blessed by her. It was amazing and inspiring to hear. Our church had a weekly time of prayer on Wednesday nights that both of us attended. It was not very structured like a church service and the group was usually no bigger than ten people. We all prayed as we felt led. Occasionally, Carolyn, of course, felt led. So she would pray. I had absolutely no idea what she said, but I heard everyone say the customary "mmmmm…" sound of agreement when she did pray, so out of peer pressure in hopes of not being the odd one out in the group, I just did the same thing.

For many years, that was my "relationship" with Carolyn. Pretty exciting, huh? I never greeted her because I was afraid of what would happen next. What would I say? How would I say it? What if she said something back? What if when she did say something back, which she probably would, I couldn't understand her? So I just let other people greet her instead. I think I was friends with her on Facebook too, so that was good enough, right?

In 2010, I started working for a national student ministry organization called the Navigators. I was connected to them through my school, Eastern Connecticut State University, while I was a student there. I was a member of a club that they were affiliated with. After graduation, I decided to join their staff as a missionary. Doing that, however, meant that I had to raise financial support and find donors to support me. I started out with a list, and Carolyn was one of the lucky winners who made it on there. Thus began my formal interactions with Carolyn. She started responding to my emails really positively and gave me some ministry connections since she worked for a nonprofit called the Council for Christian Arts.

Then in November 2010, I sent out an email to my contact list asking if they knew of anyone who had an apartment or spare room available that they might be willing to give as a gift to my ministry either for free or for a discounted amount. I was pleasantly surprised when Carolyn responded, saying she had a room available in her house that she'd rent to me for half the price. I was floored at her generosity. By the end of that month, I was all moved in.

I quickly discovered that this would not be a typical renting situation.

First of all, I was shocked to find out that Carolyn, a woman with cerebral palsy, actually owned a house. I knew that people with disabilities oftentimes lived with others, whether family members or professional aides, but I never thought that she would actually have the house in her name. There were four other people who lived in the house with us and one of them was her live-in assistant.

So Carolyn can really do immensely more than most think she can do, but she still needs the occasional helping hand. How it would go is that I would usually be in the kitchen prepping dinner or a snack or something, then I would hear a *click, click-click, click*, followed by the slow roll of Carolyn's electric wheelchair creeping across her wooden floor. I would then hear a tiny utterance of "Steve…"

I'd turn around and see Carolyn in the doorway. "Can you help me?"

It was usually a variety of things. A typical request for midafternoon might be that she would ask if I could take her hat off. Her "hat" wasn't one she wore to be fancy. It was one she wore so she could type on the computer since she didn't really have full use of her hands. It was a device made entirely of metal with a thin circular part that wrapped around her head. Then it had another thin metal rod that stuck out and hung down across her face in front of the bridge of her nose. At the end of that rod was a little foam ball duct-taped with purple duct tape, because Carolyn is fancy like that.

She would type by maneuvering that ball toward different keys on her keyboard.

Her computer had a fancy software similar to what most phones have on text messaging. It would help her type faster by displaying different words on the screen as she typed. If it was the word she was going for, she would select it. Whenever she typed, there would be high-pitched beeps and boops that could be heard all throughout the house.

The hat also had a Velcro strap that went under her chin. That Velcro strap was always a doozy for her and she needed a helping hand with it. After I got the hat off, I'd ask where she wanted it, and she would shift and maneuver her arm to motion in the direction of her desk. I'd plop it on there, and then she would usually head outside if the day was nice, usually to read a book.

Yes, Carolyn, a woman with cerebral palsy, reads books. I was surprised about that. One book that always reminds me of her is the six-hundred-page hardcover biography *Bonhoeffer* by Eric Metaxas.

At first, my relationship with Carolyn was just the occasional greeting and request for help. I would have great conversations with her assistants. All of them were very friendly, and as I talked with them, Carolyn would also listen in and talk with me too. When she talked, her assistants would always help interpret what she was saying for me. That helped me then feel more comfortable to actually engage Carolyn in conversation.

Having a conversation with Carolyn is quite a process. It involves meticulous patience, but she will always make it worth your while. She will first say a sentence that comes slurring out of her mouth. Then I will try to guess what she says by repeating it back. If I got it right, she would continue. If I got it wrong, she would shake her head.

"Say it again?"

She would give it another shot.

"Nope. First word?"

A sound.

"Sorry. Spell it?"

First letter.

"W..."

Second letter.

"H... What?"

Nod. Repeat of first word and another.

"What are..."

Next word. Next word.

"You doing..."

Last word.

"Today? Oh, not much, just watching a movie upstairs. I might go out with a friend later."

That's how a typical conversation would go. The longer I would talk with her though, the more I found myself being able to understand her words and her actions. The conversations would shift away from shallow things like the weather and how we're doing, to topics like politics, church, friends, and life. Though at first glance Carolyn seemed limited and boring, she actually did a lot of exciting things in her life. She gave lectures at college classes, she spoke with politicians, she worked jobs, plus she did a lot of administrative work for the Council for Christian

Arts. Carolyn was an accomplished woman who was happily retired. Yes, retired.

She also owned a condo that she rented out to college students as well. She typed up the leases that they signed and met with tenants to go over details with them.

In the Book of James, we're told to be "quick to hear, slow to speak" (James 1:19). Achieving those characteristics is incredibly easy for Carolyn. She listens better than most people I know. She also has a deep well of life experience. Carolyn helped open my eyes about the life of a person with a disability.

One story I remember her telling is one time when she was visiting a church. The sermon that Sunday was incredibly moving for her and the pastor gave an altar call. Carolyn felt challenged and convicted, so she responded like anyone else would in a typical church service: she went up to the altar.

The pastor and a few others also felt moved to come up to her, lay hands on her, and start praying. However, what they started praying was not about her convictions she was feeling in her heart. Instead, it was about her disability and that God would "heal" her of it.

You want to talk about angry? She was fuming. One thing you should never do to Carolyn, or anyone with a physical/mental disability, is say that that disability is something *wrong* with them. No, it is not wrong. She's different than most people, yes, but she is not wrong.

What was even more upsetting to her that Sunday was that if she did speak up, she knew no one there would understand her. She knew the only thing it would be is to trouble them, so she did the only thing she could do. She stayed quiet and just prayed to Jesus for strength and grace.

I also learned that Carolyn is *immensely* prolife. Many doctors would try to pressure a potential mother of a child like Carolyn to terminate that pregnancy. The doctors would say it would be better for the child not to live with all that suffering and hardship. They would say that terminating that pregnancy would, in essence, be "saving" that child. As a parent, raising a child with a disability takes work. But parents are not "putting them out of their misery" if they decide to snuff them out before they're even born. The fact of the matter is that those parents are not even giving their children a chance to live the life God is calling them to live.

As Carolyn would be sharing deeply about topics like this, she would, like most people, get pretty emotional. Her intense eyes would widen, and her body would shift back and forth with a tension that became palpable to anyone who would be conversing with her.

Yes, Carolyn has passions. Carolyn has interests. And like most people, Carolyn has a sense of humor. She is snarky and sharp-witted, right up my lane. Much of my time living under her roof has had laughter involved. I would oftentimes have my then-girlfriend-now-wife Amy over to the house, and we would be making dinner together in the kitchen. Amy and I would share a good laugh over a funny joke, and then we would hear a loud laugh from Carolyn as she was beep-booping on her computer in the room next door.

All in all, Carolyn's life is lived very simply, and in many ways, it is lived very simply for others. Every single person who comes to live under her roof or care for her or just visit her is another person she has blessed.

24

Boarders and Friends

Beloved, you do faithfully whatever you do
for the brethren and for strangers.
—3 John 1:5

Jason was leaning against the wall of the empty dining room as we discussed repairs and adjustments that
needed to be made before boarders started moving into the
house. While living at Sara's house, I placed an ad on a
University of Connecticut website that assists students in
finding off-campus houses. I would soon learn that foreign
students were drawn to this website.

I had learned quite a bit from Jason's point of view
regarding his marriage with Becky in the two weeks spent at
Sara's. Their marriage started to unravel soon after it began,
and having children in quick succession didn't help the situation. Why didn't I see it? Was I so blind, or did they hide
it well? The answers eluded me, but I knew enough not
to enter the blame game. Actually, it's not a game, but a
serious flaw in human nature. It started in the Garden of

Eden with Adam and Eve disobeying God by eating the fruit from the tree in the middle of the garden. The serpent tempted Eve by twisting her word. When God confronted them, that's when the blaming began, and we have been doing it ever since with small and great consequences.

Jason did some maintenance to get the house ready for boarders. There were four bedrooms on the second floor, two of which were small. The smaller of the two Jason had used for an office; the other was Nic's bedroom. For rental purposes, the two rooms were combined. Doorknobs were changed on each of the bedroom doors to allow for privacy for the tenants. The door to the sunporch was fixed so nobody could break in from the back of the house. Cookie had taken most of the furniture and kitchen utensils. A trip or two to the Salvation Army thrift shop was a big help in suppling needed items. Jason and Aaron did the heavy lifting to get the couch, dining room table, and other items in the door and placed properly.

The first "takers" were a couple from Bangladesh. Kazi was a doctoral student at the University of Connecticut in the engineering field. He was wearing the usual T-shirt and mid-thigh shorts. He had been in the area for a year or two. His wife, Sharman, was a newcomer to the United States but spoke English fairly well. She wore a colorful traditional sari. She had the ambition of obtaining her doctorate in medical research. I was taken aback when Kazi started to negotiate the amount of the rent. It finally occurred to me this was what they did in their culture.

Throughout their one-and-a-half-year stay, Sharman cooked several Bangladeshi dishes. Some were a tad too spicy for my tongue. She was in the kitchen every day. Every so often she would deliver a dish to my kitchenette. One of my favorites was tuna balls. They had all kinds of spices mixed into the balls.

By the time the fall semester began in September, all the rooms were filled, mostly with foreign students. With some, like Kazi and Sharman, there was regular interaction, and others were absorbed in their studies. The atmosphere seemed more like a boarding house than a home. Although the renters were friendly, there was an aloofness.

On a few occasions, I felt a twinge of culture clash. Sharman had asked me if they could have some guests over for dinner during Ramadan. Although Ramadan is the most holy holiday for the Muslims, involving prayer and fasting, the last few days of it are a celebration in the evening after sunset. Wanting to accommodate, I quickly agreed. The night of the celebration and fasting, I laid in bed feeling a bit uncomfortable. This was a free country where freedom of religion is of primary importance. Kazi, Sharman, and the other renters were guests in the house. I should willingly respect their faith, which I did. But this house was meant to be dedicated to the Lord of Abraham, Isaac, and Jacob. They were honoring the God of Abraham, Ishmael, and Mohammed. I came to the conclusion, after some wrestling in my spirit, that Jesus would have mercy, compassion, and forgiveness with the situation.

Candy popped back into my life after some time of not hearing from her. She wanted me to meet her new husband, Russell. The maroon oriental-patterned wallpaper border I had selected for the kitchenette/dining area wasn't put up yet. Candy had experience putting up borders and quickly selected Russel to assist her in pasting the border on the wall just below the celling. The border brightened up the room, and I was thankful for their hard work.

A few months again passed before Candy came to the house with an idea. She thought of forming a ladies' group that would share, support, and pray for each other. Of course, there had to be food. So the informal Friday night prayer dinner began, gathering together weekly. Although she wasn't attending Abundant Life anymore, she thought of several women from the church whom she would like to invite to join us, including Nikki, Donna, and Debbie.

Nikki was a woman who had been through a difficult divorce. Her daughter and two sons were in various stages of walking away from the Lord, which grieved her heart. Her talents lie in working with children and caring for seniors. She had a bachelor's degree in art and used various styles of paintings. Debbie and Donna, in one sense, had similar backgrounds. Both were in recovery, had difficult childhood memories, and had failed marriages. Their personalities were quite different. Debbie was a seeker of God who asked many questions and struggled to understand the answers. Donna, on the other hand, was laid-back and easygoing. The five of us would make up the core of the group. Over the years that followed, many people have joined us. Some come one or two times. Others join us regularly for a while.

In the fall of 2010, the type of renters started to shift from foreign students who would stay for a semester or two then move on with their lives to persons from the community, primarily with some Christian-faith background.

The first to begin this trend was Donna. Lynn had made a connection with her a year or two earlier while she was living in a sober house. On several occasions, my assistant and I would pick her up to bring her to church as I lived closer to the sober house than anyone attending the church. She was always polite and appreciative, but didn't say much. Penny, a friend from church who was beginning to mentor Donna, had her give me a call because she was looking for a more permanent place to live. Little did anyone know how permanent the living arrangement would be. Although I've moved to a different location, as of this writing, Donna still lives with me.

Not long after Donna moved into the house, a mutual relationship began to develop. Donna had, and still has, a giving heart and began to take care of my physical needs. She had her own needs for guidance and direction in making both small and large decisions. Due to abuse as a child and unhealthy sexual relationships in her past, she needed encouragement from those around her. Some days are more challenging for her emotionally than others.

Slowly, over time and with the Lord's help, she has improved her emotional stability. There were several times when it felt like she'd taken two steps forward and one step back. We would encourage her with godly advice and remind her she was a child of God.

Sheila was one of many who spoke words of encouragement into Donna's life, along with some suggestions for correction. Shelia had graduated from Teen Challenge after two years of what she nicknamed Jesus's boot camp. She stayed in an old trailer behind Sara's house. As the weather got cooler and basement space became available, she decided to move in. She always livened up a place with her active, creative mind, which reminded me of a whirlwind.

One evening during Bible study, Steve, a student at Eastern Connecticut State Universality in Willimantic, mentioned he wanted to move closer to campus. I had admired his quick wit, friendly but reserved personality, and his eagerness to know more and tell people, particular young Eastern students, about Jesus. He was so serious about proclaiming Jesus that he was a part-time missionary on campus for the Navigators. After praying that night, I pursued obtaining contact information to see if he would be interested in a room that just became available.

A few months after settling in, he met Amy, who was a UConn student who just happened to walk into Abundant Life Church one Sunday morning. It was a God-ordained visit. Amy was a sweet, seemingly shy girl with curly dark red hair and who had a holy boldness for telling strangers about Jesus. She also had a part-time ministry position on campus, but hers was with Campus Crusade for Christ. A relationship grew between them and began to blossom around the kitchen table in the main part of the house.

There were a few interesting conversations between Kazi and Steve discussing and comparing similarities and differences with the Muslim beliefs and Christianity. I listened in on the conversation and contributed a thought or two. We seemed to skirt around the fundamental issue of Jesus being the Son of God.

Kazi and Sharmin lived in the house a little over a year. During that time, they had a big event in their lives.

A few months after they settled into their two small rooms, Sharmin announced she was pregnant. Kazi was grinning from ear to ear the day they brought their baby girl, Zaima, home from the hospital and presented her to me before bringing her upstairs to their rooms. It was striking when I heard Kazi refer to himself as "aba" when taking to Zaima. I instantly thought of Jesus calling His heavenly Father, Abba. In America, we don't realize that some ancient words used in biblical times are still used today in the Middle East.

Some friends of Kazi and Sharmin's offered the use of their apartment. The fall semester had ended, and they were moving on, but the lease for the apartment had a few more months before it ended. On a cold January day, Kazi loaded my van several times over with their belongings to make the six-mile trip over to their new apartment on Foster Drive.

There was no need to advertise "room for rent" when Kazi and Sharmin left. Angie had already expressed interest in renting the two small rooms for her and her teenage son, Bryant. Angie and I had gotten to know each other when she volunteered to drive me to see Sheila, sometimes bringing Sheila's daughter, Jocelyn, with us.

It was always an adventure going to and from Providence, Rhode Island, to see Sheila while she lived at Teen Challenge. One could tell crossing the state line eastbound on Route 6 that there were potholes every few feet or some kind of roadway constitution going on. My van was lower to the ground than most vehicles due to the hydraulic system used to operate the ramp. The ramp allows me access to the van by maneuvering my motorized wheelchair. Many times, when we hit a pothole, the bottom of the van would hit the cement, commonly known as bottoming out. When Angie would come to take me to visit Sheila, she would ask, "Are you ready for a roller-coaster ride?"

Angie was a jokester. One winter, we had snowstorm after snowstorm. She threatened to attached a snowplow to the front of my wheelchair so I could help shovel. She even found a cartoon character on the Internet that was in a wheelchair with a plow in front of it.

Sheila had moved to a local campground in the summer. Through her connections, she heard of a woman named Kim who had just come out of Teen Challenge and was looking for a place to live.

When Angie moved in, she in a way completed the house—all of us living in it were practicing Christians. There was a sense of caring for one another and having a commonality with one another. Although we had different personalities and various things ticked us off, we all had the same foundation.

Hurricanes, like snowstorms, are part of life living in New England. In late August of 2011, Hurricane Irene struck Connecticut with a mighty force. Gale winds were up to sixty miles per hour at the peak of the storm, a little less where we were. We were without electricity for a week. This meant no running water. Toilets had to be flushed by pouring water in the tank when necessary. Taking showers at the Mansfield Community Center was an inconvenience, but I was grateful it was available.

Several of us headed to the community center the first evening they were serving meals, but by the third dinner, we had had enough. It seemed to be similar foods night after night. Creative Angie offered to make the evening meal for everyone. We lingered at the table on the sunporch, telling stories about our family and friends, knowing there was not much to do after dark without electricity.

After approximately a year of tabletop conversations, Steve popped the big question, and Amy answered in the affirmative. The Abundant Life family was invited, and Pastor Kevin conduct the ceremony where Steve's parents went to church. Our whole house was invited to the wedding, plus all my personal assistants. It was a simple gathering to unite a man and a woman as one, as God has ordained.

A few times a week, Donna and I would drive to various local places just to have a change of pace and for Donna to get some exercise. One place we frequented was Mansfield Hollow Dam State Park. This was a warm July Saturday afternoon when we meet up with Kazi, Sharmin, and little Zaima. It was a delight to see them and we started chatting. It turned out God designed our bumping into one another. They were looking for a place to live again and Steve was about to leave due to his upcoming marriage. Within a few days, I received a call confirming Kazi and his family would rent the master bedroom, which Steve was currently occupying.

Although I was glad that Kazi and Sharmin were back living in the house, not everyone was pleased. The spices from Sharmin's cooking were not appreciated, and there was a quiet competition on the use of the kitchen. They ended up only staying a semester. Kazi was delighted when a university in Idaho offered him a position in his field. He had been searching for quite a while.

There seemed to be a shift in atmosphere each time a renter moved in or out. This can be expected but can be wearing after a time. Then there is the energy, money, and worry about finding new tenants. On one hand, it piqued my interested when a student from a foreign land would share their stories. On the other hand, it was disturbing to hear what I consider immoral behavior happening right above my head.

Usually I celebrate Thanksgiving with Glen, Kathi, and their children and grandchildren. In 2014, they were invited to spend the day with a man Marj had met after she moved to New Hampshire with her son, Wyatt. Sara heard about my plight and invited me to join her family for Thanksgiving dinner. While Sara was eating and feeding me, I popped an unexpected question to her. "What do you think about me moving to the campground?" Her surprised look quickly turned into excitement. A year or two before, she had a tiny house given to her by a woman who lived at the campground.

"Oh, there is a house diagonally across from my hobbit house that might work out for you," she replied.

"A few nights ago," I went on to explain, "I was in bed worrying and praying when all of sudden the thought entered my head, 'Move to the campground.' It had to be from the Lord."

I had been on the grounds of the Willimantic Camp Meeting Association (WCMA) during the past ten or more years. The Council for Christian Arts had collaborated with the WCMA on several occasions to bring local musicians together for a concert and bring a few more well-known ministries, like the Sky Family, to WCMA. Several members of my church family lived on the grounds of WCMA and would invite the congregation to events.

To confirm I was heading in the direction God wanted me to go, I asked for Pastor Kevin's thoughts. In the past, I've made decisions without consulting with wise Christian leaders, which had gotten me into trouble. A few weeks later, at the beginning of a fellowship meal after Sunday service, he came behind my wheelchair, leaned over, and whispered in my ear, "It will be fine, apply." That was the go-ahead I needed to apply for membership at WCMA.

All kinds of cleaning and preparations were made before the final move. From the prompting of the Holy Spirit to the day of the big move, it was exactly a year.

There was one last event to take place in the blue house—the surprise celebration of Debbie's birthday. In addition to the usual people during Friday dinner gathering, the Abundant Life family came, and all brought delicious dishes to share. After Debbie's initial surprise, a round of thank-yous and lots of *oohs* and *aahs*, she exclaimed, "Nobody has ever given me a birthday party, not even my mother." There was a moment's pause, then we dug into the tasty food, which all enjoyed. What would a birthday party be without presents and cake made by Sara Sabo.

Debbie raved about the chocolate and vanilla cake with light cream frosting and the entire evening for months.

Reflecting on the evening's events in bed that night, I pondered Debbie's statement. I couldn't imagine growing up and not having your family celebrate your birthday. She had told of her dysfunctional upbringing and how it continued throughout her adult life. For the majority of her life, she had lived in a world far different from what I had known. A world with love. A world with Jesus.

EPILOGUE

On November 21, 2015 (Glen's birthday), I moved into a house built in 1910, which needed renovations to accommodate my needs. Ironically, I bought the house on my birthday. Thanks to Glen, Kathi, and the Abundant Life family, the day of the move went smoothly. The very next Wednesday, I was able to join a Bible study that met on the campgrounds.

Donna and I enjoy living in this Christian community where most people know one another. As soon as we moved in, Sara made sure her son, JD, built a ramp by her back door. We have access to each other's houses at any time.

During the pandemic, I was blessed, as I usually am, with good health. When the pandemic first started, one of my personal assistants chose to isolate at home as was recommend by health and government officials. The Lord immediately provided Joy, who was from the Philippines. She had needed a place to live in a few months prior and had found one with Sara. She was more than happy to fill in, and her bubbly personality brightened up the house each time she came.

In January, when the pandemic was at one of its peaks, I was exposed to it in my own home. I was tested positive but had no symptoms. Unfortunately, Donna did have symptoms plus had to take care of my daily needs while being sick because we were all in quarantine. It was a great blessing, thanks to my good friend Penny, to have meals delivered at our door by various people from Abundant Life.

The journey of life will continue on this earth until we are called home by the Creator of the universe. I know where I'm going. Do you?

GIVE THANKS

*Give thanks in all circumstances; for this is God's will
for you in Christ Jesus.*

—1 Thessalonians 5:18

There is a wise godly woman I know who each time someone asks "how are you" she replies, "thankful." After hearing her reply a few times, I thought to myself, *That's truly the way to live, to be thankful in all things.*

First, I give thanks to my family. Mom was an amazing woman who, for the majority of my growing up years, raised us alone. Before "inclusion" was a buzz word, my family included me in family milestones as well as everyday activities. More importantly, they gave me a firm foundation and the freedom to make my own choices.

Many thanks go to Diane, Dianna, Donna, and many others throughout the years who have assisted me in the activities of daily living. They all have unique giftings and a special place in my heart. I'm especially grateful for Cleo Pearl who has assisted me in getting out of bed, my daily routine, and millions other things. Her loyalty and love over thirty-five years have been amazing.

This book would not be written without the persistent encouragement and nagging of my dear friend, Sara Sabo. She would say "People need to know these things." She would become infuriated when strangers would treat me like a child.

I'm grateful for the many hours of editing and word-smithing Lynn White did before it went to the publisher. Her suggestions and encouragement were much appreciated. The love of God she has for everyone she meets is an example to all.

A big thank you to Beverly Woodcock, Pastor Kevin White, Steve Timmons, and Candy Wilks for the time and creativity it took to write a chapter for this book. They add different perspectives to the book and give it character. Christian Faith Publishers saw the potential of *Choices and Wheels* which I'm grateful for. Their encouraging staff are helpful and professional.

ABOUT THE AUTHOR

Growing up, Carolyn Newcombe occasionally wondered what life had in store for her. Due to a lack of oxygen at birth, she has lived with a condition called cerebral palsy. Although she had a supportive family, some professionals expressed low expectations for her life.

Choices and Wheels tells of her triumphs and successes, as well as her failures and foibles. Through her faith in Jesus, she realizes that human beings have many common characteristics no matter our race, cultural background, the language we speak, or the disability we experience. God has given each one of us the gift of life. With His strength and direction, Carolyn Newcombe is an example of this principle by her perseverance, love of people, and respect for the Word of God.

A disability does give you a perspective on certain things. Every person perceives circumstances differently, depending on their experiences in life. Sprinkled throughout the book are stories of the reaction of individuals to her disability. The last third of *Choices and Wheels* has some chapters written by friends to give you, the reader, another perspective.

Her purpose in writing this book is twofold—to demonstrate that God can and does use anyone, whether they have a disability or not, to accomplish his purposes and to give you a tiny taste of life living with a physical disability. Her prayer is that your view of life will be enriched and that your view of people with disabilities will be expanded.

9 781639 614028